FRENCH DIRT

FRENCH

DIRT : THE STORY

OF A GARDEN

IN THE

SOUTH OF FRANCE

RICHARD GOODMAN

Algonquin Books of Chapel Hill

1991

Published by

Algonquin Books of Chapel Hill

Post Office Box 2225

Chapel Hill, North Carolina 27515-2225

a division of

Workman Publishing Company, Inc.

708 Broadway

New York, New York 10003

LIBRARY OF CONGRESS CATALOGING-IN-PUBLICATION DATA

Goodman, Richard

French dirt : the story of a garden in the south

of France / Richard Goodman.—1st ed.

p.   cm.

ISBN 0-945575-66-1

1. Vegetable gardening—France, Southern.

2. Goodman, Richard.

I. Title.

SB320.8.F7G66   1991

635'.0944—dc20   91-120 CIP

10 9 8 7 6 5 4 3 2 1

FIRST EDITION

 TO IGGY

I. THE VILLAGE

Acknowledgements

Certain people have helped me tremendously in writing this book. They are: Shannon Ravenel, Abby Thomas, Ron Arnold, Dodds Musser, Bettye Dew and Donna Van Buren. I thank them very much. Most of all, I want to thank Deborah Attoinese, filmmaker *extraordinaire,* unerring critic and best friend, for giving so much, so often.

A Note about Names . . .

When I came to the place I call St. Sébastien de Caisson, I had no idea that I would ever have a garden, much less write about one. Now that I have done just that, I think it only right that I change the name of the village and the villagers themselves. The villagers spoke to me unguardedly, without any idea that their words might someday appear in print. I feel I must respect their openness of heart, and their privacy, by keeping their identities hidden.

. . . And about Gardens and Gardeners

In St. Sébastien de Caisson, my village, the gardeners, with only a few exceptions, were men. Mostly older men, too, those who were semiretired from working in the vineyards and who had enough time to dedicate to the task of raising zucchini, tomatoes, eggplant and all the other vegetables that were planted. (I should say that whenever I speak of gardens, I mean vegetable gardens.) They tended their gardens with care, and the results were always wonderful to see. Each garden in its own way was different, but they were all successful. In the course of my time in St. Sébastien, I talked to most of the men and to the few women who had gardens. They were consistently generous with their advice, and also highly opinionated. For them, gardening was serious. It was not an amusement. It provided food. I tried not to forget that.

Intimacy with another country is ripened by pleasures but also by loneliness and error.

—Shirley Hazzard, "Italian Hours"

 FRENCH DIRT

 PROLOGUE

THIS IS A LOVE STORY. Like most love stories,
it has its share of joy and passion, of loss and pain.
Like most love stories, it also has its moments of
melodrama, of emotions run amok, of suspicions,
worries, anxieties, of pride and panic—of jealousy,
even. And, like many familiar love stories, it has
times of great pleasure and bliss, only to end, because
fate or the gods willed it, cataclysmically.

In this case, the object of my love was not a
woman. It was a small, rectangular piece of land in
the south of France.

This is the story of my garden.

 THE VILLAGE

INSPIRATION

I HAD A GARDEN in the south of France. It wasn't a big garden. Or a sumptuous one. Or a successful one, even, in the end. But that didn't matter. It was my garden, and I worked it hard and lovingly for the few months I had it—or it had me. This little piece of tan, clayey, French earth, nine meters by thirteen meters, (thirty feet by forty-three feet), was in fact the first garden I ever had. It taught me a great deal about myself. "Your garden will reveal yourself," writes the wise gardener Henry Mitchell. It did. It taught me that I am generous, impatient, hard-working, sentimental, boyish, stubborn and lazy.

Having a garden also connected me to France in a way more profound and more lasting than any other way I can possibly think of. Part of me is still there. And always will be. Even though my friend Jules Favier has recently written to me from the village that "only one of the four boundaries of your garden remains standing," I'm not upset. What does that matter? The garden is in my heart. Having a garden gave me a *place* to go in my village every day, a task to perform and a responsibility. You cannot ask more of a land in which you are a stranger. To feel the French earth, clear it, plant seeds in it, despair over it and, ultimately, to take from it, that was a precious gift.

Gardeners are born *and* made, I believe. "There are no green thumbs or black thumbs," to quote Henry Mitchell again. "There are only gardeners and non-gardeners." What makes a gardener is two things: the desire to garden and a piece of land with which to satisfy that desire. The first can certainly exist, and often does, without the second. As I said, I never had a garden of my own until I was forty-three years old and living in a little wine-making village in the south of France, near Avignon. All my life I had wanted to have a garden. But I'd always managed to find myself living in large American cities in which that desire was thwarted, where every morsel of free earth was either a park or was snatched up by some developer to build a new skyscraper. The desire was always there, though, smoldering, ready to explode into being.

I live in New York City now. A good friend of mine has a house in rural Pennsylvania. I am her official gardener. Because we both know and love France, we have given me the nickname "Le Nôtre," the name of Louis XIV's famous gardener. There in Pennsylvania, I dig her wild dark ground, dislodge the hundreds of stones, then plant and weed the kind of flowers that will grow in her shadowy back yard—impatiens, marigold, so on. When I'm in New York, I yearn to be back there. I can spend an entire day working in her yard, easily. Even though the land is hers, I'm content. Ownership does not always provide freedom. In her back yard, I am lost. I am lost in my work.

I love to garden for the obvious—but, because of that, no less meaningful—reason: to feel connected to the earth and its moods, to its weather and its seasons, to its eccentricities and surprises. I love to bend and dig and pull and haul. (Just look at those words! Short, simple words. Not a prissy, ten-dollar word like *decorate* among them.) I am always searching for ways to make myself simpler. Gardening does that better than anything I know. It reduces me to who I am. It casts off the superficial and the artificial. It leaves me with the essential, the economical, the no-frills me.

I grew up in southeastern Virginia, on the ocean. I had a boyhood full of intoxicating smells, of the soft spray from the ocean, the forceful perfume of gardenias, the scent of ripe figs wafting into the open window. In the summer, it was very hot, but often there was a wind from the ocean to make the heat bearable. Everything was more intense in the sun-drenched summer: roses, the crisp grass dehydrated by the heat, fat bees languidly treading air, even the mockingbirds. Before I was old enough to go to school, I walked around barefoot from May to October. I knew every plant and bush and flower, everything that grew near our house, from all sides. There were no barriers between me and the earth. I *was* the summer.

The first gardener I ever met was a black man. His name was Ford, and he worked for my grandmother. When she came from her house in Norfolk to stay with us during the summer, Ford came, too. I was never happier than to see him arrive every May. He was a quiet, hard-working man with lovely, peat-colored skin who spent long hours in the fierce summer sun working on the plants and shrubs and flowers in our yard. He was both a father and a mother figure to me, tolerant and accepting. I used to follow him around for hours in the hot Virginia day. Remembering how hard he worked and how thoroughly—I can still see the sweat dripping down his neck and cheeks, the small veins bulging on his forehead, a bandanna curled around his neck—I'm sure I was a distraction, if not a downright nuisance. But he never excluded me. He made me feel a part of his task.

What fascinated me about Ford even as a little boy was the boldness with which he worked. He snipped and cut our peach tree so deftly and rapidly it frightened me. "Won't that kill the tree if you do that, Ford?" I asked him as he pruned the tree. "No, boy. This is going to *help* this peach tree." Branches and twigs flew off the tree with a blinding rapidity as his scissors darted here and there and everywhere. There might have been a logic somewhere, but I couldn't find it. "But, Ford, how do you know *what* to cut?" I pleaded. He bent down and cut off a huge branch. He'd cut too much! I squealed and looked down in horror at the large crooked arm, leaves still on it. Ford stood back up. "I just know, boy."

And, indeed, later that summer we had big fat pink peaches, globes hanging everywhere from that tree. And they exploded with deliciousness.

Ford taught me that life can be enhanced by death, that injury is not necessarily injury in the world of plants. But I learned something more important from him, even if I didn't quite understand it completely at the time: that there is a difference in nature between what grows purely wild and what has been tamed. And that gardening is a collaboration. Somewhere, even after I left Virginia and moved into a

7

succession of big, earthless metropolitan centers, I kept those lessons deep inside me, along with the primal memories of sun and heat and dirt and the scent-soaked summer air.

CLEARING

I DID NOT BEGIN my garden until I had been in France for six months. It wasn't until I had made a few good friends—and one special one—and had worked on land belonging to others, and had been more or less accepted in St. Sébastien. But by April I had acquired my own little plot of land. It was about a mile away from the village, near a stream, and it was waist-high with weeds. I thought it was beautiful, but it needed to be cleared.

The day that my benefactor Jules Favier came with the tractor to clear the land was a momentous one for me.

Jules had been busy in the vineyards, so it was difficult for him to liberate the tractor to help me. I wanted him there right away, of course. There was the land, waiting! I would drive by from time to time and gaze at it, just to renew my sense of belonging. Then one day about two weeks after he had first showed me the land, Jules came by my house at noon when the whole village of St. Sébastien was sitting down to eat lunch and announced he would bring the tractor to the land at four o'clock that afternoon.

As usual, he was doing this as a favor to me. And as usual, he refused to accept my gratitude. This was, as he might say, a question of *bien sûr*. Of course. Of course, I will clear your land. *That is given.*

I was there early. I parked my little Peugeot 104 at the edge of a vineyard, near the stream. It was a chilly, sunny day in late April. In the south of France, "sunny" means you have a light that is nearly three-dimensional, an eye-blinking, chrome-yellow presence that, like a remarkable personality at a party, dominates without trying. They have a name for the north wind here; they should also have a name for the sun. *Le mistral* is the name of the dreaded wind that sweeps down the Rhône valley, "this visitor," Colette writes, "for whom no sanctum is private." They might call the sun the Lion, *le Lion*. Because here it is golden and mighty. And, in the summer, predatory and merciless. Even when I had to wear my heavy leather jacket, I never felt truly cold, as long as the strong sun was there.

I slogged through the little stream—we would have to build a small bridge over that eventually—and climbed up the rise to the land. I saw the scruffy field, full of weeds and lonely-looking. For the briefest moment, I had second thoughts. But then a picture came to me. I looked, and instead of a sanctuary for weeds, I saw a garden. I saw a garden of unparalleled majesty and voluptuousness, one groaning with bounty, green and robust. One where I'd have to brush aside the thick, healthy leaves and stems to make my rounds, picking off a hock-sized zucchini here, a fistful of crisp, dirty carrots there. A garden so dense with plant life it would give off a caressing moist heat. A garden where things grew madly and happily, where I could sweat and prune and dig and water and *work*. A luscious garden of Eden. My garden!

Then I heard the sound of the tractor motor. I realized Jules would be there in a matter of moments. I looked over in the direction from where I thought the sound of the motor was coming, and when I looked back, my fabulous garden was gone. But that was all right. It would return.

The sound of the tractor grew louder. Because the way I had arrived was inaccessible to the tractor, Jules was forced to enter through his vineyard. Suddenly, from over the horizon, the tractor exploded into view. Jules arrived dramatically, driving very fast. It was a formidable machine, fierce-looking and strong, like a mantis, with its engine exposed, its huge, oversized back wheels and tiny, swerving front ones. I took a step back unconsciously in respect.

When I saw Jules there, in his blue cotton working suit, seated so authoritatively on this universal machine of work—a Massey-Ferguson—headed toward me, I felt so excited, so thrilled. There must be a unique anticipation in seeing a powerful, extraordinary machine—whether it's a tractor, bulldozer, trench digger—that is about to alter your land.

I gave Jules an oversized wave and shouted a loud greeting, as if I were welcoming home the cruise ship *Normandy*. Jules nodded, but he didn't stop. He was all business. Besides, as I knew very well, he wasn't a waver. He had a plow connected to the back of the tractor, a slick, steel blade with a pronounced curve that hovered about four inches above the ground. When he reached the edge of my future garden, he adjusted some knobs and the blade dipped into the earth. The tractor growled and Jules was off, the blade tearing into the earth. He worked his machine with great concentration, dividing his gaze between the land ahead of him and what was just behind him as the steel made a long, deep, effortless incision.

I watched transfixed as the tractor blade brought up the earth in smooth turns, like wide peels of an apple. But this was devastation! Corpulent worms were divided in half by the blade; a mouse fled across the field only inches from my feet, its home suddenly disclosed by this force; plants were completely up-rooted; debris from a decade back was exposed. The blade devoured everything. The world was literally turned upside down.

Jules worked quickly, and it seemed only a matter of minutes before he was nearly through. What had been only a level field of weeds was now a choppy brown sea. I walked a bit into the disrupted land. The serrations made me slip and totter. As Jules made a final far turn, I bent down and took a fresh, damp clump of earth in my hand. It was slick and cool, nearly odorless. It's mine, I thought.

The sun began to dip below the hills in the distance. An authentic chill would soon be over the land. I wasn't thinking of how much work there was ahead of me. I wasn't thinking of anything. I looked over at Jules and held up the beautiful glob, some severed roots dangling through my fingers. I shook it at him triumphantly as bits of earth fell down my arm. Jules looked at me and shook his head. He shook his head even as he stopped and shifted into reverse to attack a small patch of weeds the tractor had missed.

Jules had done his part. Now it was up to me. And the land.

 # THE VILLAGE

THAT MY FIRST garden should be in the south
of France in an obscure village west of Avignon may
seem a bit odd, but life can be like that. How I got
there and why I got there is a story in itself, bound up
with a transatlantic love affair and with my growing disaffection with New York, among other things.
The love affair did not have a happy ending—and is
not the subject of this book—but I would take the
journey again, anytime.

Suffice it to say that I lived in a small wine-making
village called St. Sébastien de Caisson (population
211), which is about 450 miles south of Paris, 100

miles northwest of Marseille, 35 miles west of Avignon—and 30 years behind all of them. I lived in St. Sébastien with my Dutch girlfriend, Igminia, for one year in a two-hundred-year-old stone house that used to be a silkworm nursery. In the course of that year, I planted melons, I harvested asparagus, I helped clear and prune the vineyards, I picked potatoes. And I had a garden.

The land on which St. Sébastien is located, just about in the middle of the province called the Gard, consists of subtly undulating hills, and most of it is given over to the raising of grapes. The earth itself is the color of untreated leather. It is clayey and mixed with stones, some quite huge. There are only a few trees. Most of these—small white oak, green oak and a few evergreens—are clustered on hillsides. The famous cypresses of southern France here are found mostly in the little walled cemeteries, planted by the townspeople themselves. In this small corner of France, there are no dramatic changes in the land. What you do see in a leisurely drive from village to village down one of the narrow country roads are rows and rows of small, tough vineplants, each one like the other, stretching far into the distance. They are marked off, in their tight sameness, formally and evenly with the exactitude of a military cemetery. In the spring, before they've been pruned, their fibrous branches, adorned with dull-green leaves, sprawl out insanely, like Medusa's head of snakes. These plants that live, as one farmer told me, "about as long as a man's life," dominate both the countryside and the economy of the region.

Every so often the monotony of the vineyards is broken by the appearance of a small, dull, gray stone village. A village like St. Sébastien de Caisson, where we lived. This village in France was chosen by us from all others because of the seductive power of the English language. In New York, I subscribed to a little newspaper called *Journal Français d'Amérique*, or the *French Newspaper of America*. In the classified section in back, Igminia—or Iggy, as everybody called her—saw this ad one day:

SOUTHERN FRANCE: Stone house in Village near Nîmes/Avignon/Uzes. 4BR, 2 baths, fireplace, books, desks, bikes. Perfect for writing, painting, exploring & experiencing *la France profonde*. $450 mo. plus utilities.

Iggy circled it and showed it to me. I read it, swept away by the image. France! I looked up, and I saw the look in Iggy's eyes. I had seen this look before, many times. It said, *I am going to do this*. And then I knew I had two things I must do: Make sure we had enough money to stay for a year. And pack. Less than nine months later, at ten-thirty on a moonlit September evening, we were standing before the stone house in this small world within France, the town submerged in a disquieting silence, trying to find exactly what key fit into what door.

It is difficult to describe the ways of a village like St. Sébastien, mainly because they are so unlike what you are probably predisposed to think of when "France" is mentioned. Nevertheless, I should try to convey those ways, because they are very important to the story of my garden. Perhaps conjuring up a farm town in northern Michigan might help. I pick that not for the cold, but because, in my experience at least, such a Michigan town would be isolated, conservative and aloof. St. Sébastien is like that. It is remarkably self-contained. It is a village in which some families have been living for over four hundred years—perhaps longer, but the village's written records don't go back any farther—and where people have been doing the same thing for generations: making wine.

It is a village so small it doesn't even have a café. Or a bakery. Or a butcher shop. The number of Catholics is too small for the village to support its own priest; every six weeks a traveling priest who journeys from village to village comes to say mass at the tiny church here. It has no post office. No doctor. No gas station. No shop of *any* kind; only itinerant shops come to the village. In the mornings, small trucks, *camions,* pull into the square, blasting their shrill horns to let the villagers know they've arrived.

There is a butcher truck, fish truck, bread truck, fruit truck, even a truck that sells shoes. I think it's quite appropriate that the shopkeepers must come to St. Sébastien. It is a place in which there is little concern for the outside world—that is, for any place other than St. Sébastien de Caisson. Politics escape it, except for its own. It finds its own affairs endlessly fascinating. Balzac said it simply, and he was right: "A peasant sees nothing beyond his own village." Everything about St. Sébastien suggests the uneventful, and the eternal.

When you talk about St. Sébastien, you must eventually get a word or two in about wine. The wine made here, mostly red and rosé, is not exceptional— God help me if they ever read this in St. Sébastien!— though certainly acceptable. Even the man who runs the *cave coopérative*—that large old building whose dark, quiet, vaulted interior resembles an Ivy League boathouse, and where all the grapes are brought to be made into wine—acknowledges "it will never be Côtes-du-Rhône." The wine is sold in bulk to a large supermarket chain, which in turn sells it under its own label in five-liter plastic containers. You could often see the supermarket's long, sleek stainless-steel tankers parked next to the *cave,* gorging themselves on St. Sébastien's wine. The villagers make a decent living selling their wine. Indeed, no one in St. Sébastien is truly poor, and a few are very well off.

Right now, as I write, it is Sunday morning. I

know, with the time difference, that it is Sunday afternoon in St. Sébastien. I know exactly what is happening there now. I know it with all the certainty as I know anything. And I can see it all in my mind's eye. The villagers have had their large Sunday meal, begun precisely at noon, and are now resting. I know that the square is empty, leaving a beautiful starkness, and that the village is dead still. The responsibility of work, which normally hovers overhead like a jealous husband, is gone. The afternoon air is sweet and calm. Even such a resolute place as St. Sébastien feels sensual at this indolent afternoon hour.

I know that in a matter of minutes Madame Lécot will hurriedly emerge from her house on the square with a pail full of scrub water, her sleeves rolled up, ready to work even on Sunday. I know that Diego, the town plumber, who is the small, rapid-speaking son of Monsieur and Madame Vasquez, will soon arrive in his van. He will get out, stretch widely, light a cigarette; then he will lean against his van and wait. I know that Madame Noyer will be on her terrace now, busy with her many potted flowers. She will note his arrival with a brief pause in her work. I know that, as if by some prearranged signal, three or four more cars will now pull up and park near Diego's van. Men will get out languidly and, almost as soon as the car doors are shut, animated words will begin. The conversation is among men who have seen each other every day of their lives since they were babies. The talk—

fierce, theatrical French—will rebound off the thick walls that surround the square, return to this little group, and add to the hubbub. It will be about hunting, or the soccer game to be played later at a nearby village by these same young men, or about fishing, all according to what time of year it is. It will end just as abruptly as it began, with a few waves of the hand, doors opened and shut, cars disappearing in a dusty swirl. The square, for at least a moment, will again be dead still.

I know, now that the square is empty, that Monsieur Valcoze will take the opportunity to wander in. His task will be to survey a scene he has known, and seen virtually unchanged, for the past sixty years. I know he'll be wearing baggy pants, a cotton plaid shirt buttoned up to his throat, an old, dark cardigan and, most singularly, a battered beret. He will stand there, shifting about, his bad hip worrying him. Monsieur Valcoze is a little stout, with a haggard worker's face, which will be unshaven today. He will move his small eyes to and fro, looking. He is a solitary man, and so his intense surveying always carries with it a bit of the wasteful; it can't be a companion he is looking for. Nevertheless, how serious he looks there by himself, surveying all this emptiness! After a while, finding nothing, his hand moving against his chin, he will turn and make a long, reluctant exit.

I know what will soon follow, every detail, as if I were there myself, watching as I often did from my lofty second-story window, which overlooked the square. I know it as I know my own name, the pace and the rhythm of the village, unalterable and secure. It is as reliable and continuous as the swallows that dipped and banked sharply in their great, endless dance above the square, present day after day, year after year, stretching as far back and as far forward as the mind can conceive.

I know that at five o'clock, the *Foyer des Amis*, the Friends' Club, the closest thing St. Sébastien has to a café, will open its doors. All the men and boys and some of the women will gather there for a few hours to talk and drink and play cards and work the hand-held soccer game. For a brief time, there will be a sense of unity in St. Sébastien de Caisson. Then, almost as if embarrassed by this closeness, people will start to leave, and the day will begin its decline. When the *Foyer* closes at eight, and the last person goes home, the square will again be empty, this time for good. There will be a slight feeling of melancholy in the air as the deserted square is slowly buried in darkness.

I know these things about St. Sébastien, but I'll never truly be a part of it. I'll never really be a part of that stubborn, isolated existence I was dropped into, like a parachutist from another planet, into that life that is so much like a heartbeat. It is a life that just goes on and on, exuding a kind of simple strength, and it heeds only the most awesome forces. I may not be a part of St. Sébastien, but it certainly is a part of me.

This is the village that I surprised for a few passing months with my garden. Surprised, and was surprised by the villagers' reaction in turn—an unequal mixture of indifference, curiosity and concern.

It was just as much St. Sébastien's garden as it was my own.

 IGNORANCE

I SAID THAT COMING to St. Sébastien de Caisson
was like being parachuted into another planet, and it
is true. We flew from Manhattan directly to Paris and
were driven by Iggy's parents straight to the village,
arriving at ten-thirty in the evening to an empty
main square and a village so eerily quiet it seemed
abandoned. *Was* it abandoned, we wondered, as we
unloaded the car in the blackness? Had all the people
fled for some unknown reason? It had that strong a
feeling of emptiness.

That the villagers had already gone to bed and

were fast asleep seemed unlikely to our urban minds. But that was the case.

Two days later, when Iggy's parents had to go back to Holland and when we had finished with the diversions of unpacking and nosing around the new house, we realized how interesting a position we were in. What a great adventure to be here, how astounding.

But we knew nothing.

We didn't even know where we were. Oh, we had a map. And we knew we were in the south of France. But none of the snaking lines that led, on the bright paper spread out before us, to little villages with names like Mejannes-Sarden, Quissac, St. Paul-les-Fonts or Alès meant anything to us. Where were *they*? What use was a map? We didn't know enough geography to be lost.

We didn't know where a grocery store was. We didn't know where to buy a newspaper. Or a roll of toilet paper. (I didn't even know how to *say* toilet paper in French.) Or laundry soap. We didn't know where to mail a letter, or how to receive one; the house had no mailbox of any kind. We didn't have a bank, and had no way to draw money. We didn't have a car; we needed to rent one. We didn't even know how big the village was.

We didn't know anybody, either.

We were completely ignorant. But it is not so bad to get a good jolt in your life every once in a while. And the humbling we received from this new and strange culture, with the challenge of a language that's as difficult to speak well and correctly as any on earth, gave us a very healthy jolt indeed. One that, in the end, helped us in ways that still resonate today. While this fumbling in the dark brought with it frustration and even some panic, it also brought an ever-present sense of discovery. And adventure.

We had tried to prepare ourselves for this year. We had done our reading and research. We had interrogated as many French people and travelers as we could. But nothing could prepare us, really. For the immense quiet at night. The vast sky. The light— whose clarity and force prompted me to reach for paints I didn't have. For the view of the sloping vineyards from our bedroom window. For the subtle morning air. For marvelous tastes, the lack of distance between the sun and what you put into your mouth. For the sheer difference in living.

Waking up early in the large room, those first days, seeing Iggy beside me, I would often be disoriented, wondering exactly *where* I was. I would step down on the cool stone tiles and go to the window to look outside. I saw below me in the square the sweep of French rural life unfolding in a pure day. It was beautiful and simple, and I'd watch for minutes at a time, but at times I couldn't trust my senses. It seemed a dream.

I wanted to explore the village first. So the morning after Iggy's parents left, I set out to prowl through this village of 211 people with the strange, tripartite name.

With just 211 people, you would think my tour would be over in a matter of minutes. Would you believe me if I told you that even after a year I wasn't sure where half the people lived and to whom half the houses belonged? The village seemed to sprawl out from itself, on and on. Houses shared common walls, and it was often hard to determine where one began and the other ended. What you thought was the front door to a house was not necessarily a front door at all, or even a door belonging to that particular house. Boundaries were blurred, except to those with the experience to see them. When I walked out of our house, crossed the square and then entered a little side street that went between houses, I entered a fluid, nearly seamless world.

The houses I passed on my first walk were made of stone and most, though not all, were covered by a dull-colored plaster. When it came to their houses, the people of St. Sébastien were not preoccupied with color. Everything was made of stone—the houses, roads, walls—and so as I walked in St. Sébastien, my feet made a clacking sound. When I stepped onto one of the narrow side roads, the noise resounded off the high walls. In the dead of winter, I was to find this a lonely sound. My dark shadow striding before me on the stone would be of no comfort. Some houses had big curved doors made of ancient planks. I would later hear their boisterous racket; every so often I'd be strolling along and be surprised by the scraping and creaking as one of them labored open before me.

That warm September day, I walked carefully up and around the few winding streets of St. Sébastien. The streets ascended, and it was clear the village was built on a small hill. I tried to take everything in. An older woman walked out of her house, regarded me, and before I had a chance to say my first *bonjour,* she had locked her door and was off, her feet clacking down to the square. I walked up a small rise, and banked around a corner. Several children were playing. I said *bonjour* to them. They said, "*Quoi?*"—What?—to me and ran off. I continued.

Many of the stone houses had balconies, oftentimes overflowing with bright, beautiful flowers, some of them growing from vines with tresses that nearly touched the ground. As I gazed at one, three children looked at me from around a corner, giggled and ran off. An old man hobbled up from behind me and passed by without looking up. It was about ten o'clock. In the open, the day was beginning to feel warm, but deep within the village, the sun blocked by the wall of houses, I was cool. All of a sudden a *mobilette,* or small motorbike, whizzed by me, missing me by a foot. I jumped, my anger rising. My New York sensibility nearly took over, but I checked myself. I was to adjust in many ways that year, to retune my psychic motor, so to speak.

I somehow emerged at the very edge of the village, on top of a hill. A small road led away from St. Sébastien, and I walked on it for a while. There were a few houses along the road; sometimes a fenced-in dog would leap and shout at me, without warning, taking a few weeks off my life. After a while, I stopped and looked back. I saw that St. Sébastien was literally surrounded by vineyards, field after field, each a different shading of light green. Once I left the twisty, shadowy confines of St. Sébastien, the land dominated. It was magnificently prominent. The village was a stone island that rose up out of a body of rolling vineyards.

I walked back to the house. This time I took a different route. Glancing into windows, seeking all the information I could gather, I descended slowly. I reached the main square and walked over to the cream-colored *mairie,* or town hall. I stopped and read the notices on the glass-protected bulletin board next to the door. I saw something about electricity. I wasn't sure if the notice said it would be shut off for a few hours the next week. There was also something about taxes. No one else was about. I looked up at the building.

I didn't know then that I would come to spend many hours upstairs, pouring over the town's handwritten archives that began in the early seventeenth century, tracing generation after generation, seeing the whole history of the village flow before my eyes.

That I would in a sense witness all the births, marriages and deaths, all sparsely reported, while trying to read between the lines and *sense* the life the villagers led. I didn't know then that I would trace the name "Caisson," of St. Sébastien de Caisson, two thousand years to its Roman origin. Or that I would determine *which* St. Sébastien (of the possible five or six) the village had been named after. Who could tell me I would come to know these things, and that Iggy and I would make enduring friends here and that I would toil in the French dirt?

I turned and walked toward our house on the other side of the square. Iggy was sitting on a stone bench outside, her head tilted back against the stone wall, her eyes closed, taking in the sun. Dutch people love the sun so much! They not only grow flowers so well, they're like flowers themselves, seeking the sun whenever and however they can, their faces turned upward at the briefest appearance of the shining orb. I sat down beside her.

I saw how alone we were. Sitting on that bench, the single object in the square, I felt a bit as if we were adrift on a sea, on a flat, gray, stone sea.

 ESPAÑA

I THINK EVERY FRENCH VILLAGE should
have at least one Spanish couple living there. They
would bring a certain openness and heart—a *musi-
cality* to the village that would make it a richer place
in which to live. In St. Sébastien de Caisson, this was
provided by a couple from the province of Valencia, a
mason and his wife, Monsieur and Madame Vasquez.
They were our first friends in St. Sébastien.

In Lebanon once, years before the civil wars, I met
a young Jordanian law student. He and I were staying
at the same third-class hotel in Beirut. He befriended
me, acting as my guide and interpreter. "Why?" I

asked him once, since his unending kindness seemed excessive. "We are all strangers sometime, Richard," he said. Those first few weeks when Iggy and I were isolated and uncertain, when we were overly polite to people we didn't know and when we were pretending to be capable, Monsieur Vasquez and his wife befriended us. They took us *in*. No two people were kinder to us during that year in France. I was very grateful they were there.

Those beginning days, I would take long walks every morning. Each time I walked out of our house, I seemed to see the same short, stocky man seated on the stone bench nearby. He wasn't doing anything, just sitting. Didn't he work? I wondered. I decided to use the excuse of needing to rent a car to begin conversation. Our plan was to drive a rented car to different villages in search of a used one which we would buy.

I walked over to the bench. "Good day," I said.

"Good day," he said and squinted up at me.

"Do you happen to know," I asked him, "where I could rent a car?"

He looked to the side as if he hadn't heard me. I wondered if I'd said the sentence correctly in French. I thought I had, especially since it was one I'd practiced upstairs in our house.

"Oh," he said, "to rent a car you have to go to Alès." His accent was strange. He rolled his *r*s. I didn't know then he was Spanish.

"Alès? Is that far?"

He looked away again. "Oh, it's not far."

"Uh, how far?" I sat down cautiously next to him.

"Oh, twenty kilometers. Maybe twenty-five."

"Ah," I said. "Is there a bus that can take us there?"

"No." He paused. "There is no bus to Alès." He squinted his eyes as he looked at me.

"We need to rent a car," I said almost to myself. I was thinking aloud now. "I don't know how to get to Alès." I figured I would just hitchhike. Why not? At least I'd get to know the roads.

"Oh," he said, shifting slightly on the bench as if something was disturbing him, "I can take you."

And he did.

He did more than that, too. He took us to his house, and he introduced us to his wife. He asked us for a drink. He asked us to dinner. And to lunch. We accepted every invitation readily. And when we came, both of them talked and talked and talked. And *we* talked to *them,* ceaselessly it seemed, breathlessly telling them everything we could think of, as if we'd been lost in the mountains in the cold, and they were our rescuers. Which indeed they were.

This was only the beginning of their kindness. Now we had friends, thanks to their big Spanish hearts. I never forgot that first kind gesture to us, the strangers.

Going to the Vasquezes' house for a visit—it was

a small, cluttered, oddly-built, dark stone house just off the main square—was like going to Spain. It was always a festive occasion and always meant food and *pastis* and talk and laughter. We could drop in unannounced, and often did, spending hours at a time seated in their kitchen gossiping and exchanging information about the village. And learning.

Madame Vasquez was the larger of the couple. She was heavy, with a flat, Velázquez-like forehead, closely cropped black hair, small eyebrows and a small mouth. She always wore black, in homage to a brother who had died a few years back, but this gesture of respect was often accomodated with just a black sweater, allowing her more latitude with the rest of her wardrobe. When she laughed, she closed her eyes as if she were in pain, and her whole body trembled. She was gossipy and held grudges in a small way and enjoyed complaining. She didn't have a mean bone in her ample body. It was she, not her husband, who worked and cared for the enormous garden they maintained by the river at the edge of the village. It was unusual for a woman to tend a garden in St. Sébastien de Caisson, especially a garden so immense. But her situation made it necessary. She was a Spanish earth mother.

Monsieur Vasquez was a compact, brown-haired man with a weathered face that had been—to judge from his wedding photograph which hung on the kitchen wall—handsome at one time. He had been a

33

mason, the poverty of his native country urging him to France some twenty years ago. He had built his life in St. Sébastien from virtually nothing. A number of years before we knew him, Monsieur Vasquez had fallen from a scaffolding and broken his leg. Due to improper care, the leg never healed correctly, and so he was in constant pain and limped. He bore this pain bravely, though sometimes, when we were all around his kitchen table drinking, you would see him squeeze his eyes shut and a little cry would escape his lips.

"Your leg?" I would ask.

"Yes. *Merde*. It's worse than usual. *Three* shots I had today already!" His wife administered pain-killing shots supplied by the doctor. His injury prevented him from working—even in the garden. Bending and digging were out of the question.

Monsieur Vasquez smoked heavily, unfiltered Gauloises, and both his teeth and fingers showed the effects, not to mention that he had an ugly, watery cough. The cough became so serious that he gave up smoking while we were in St. Sébastien. And he kept to it. He chewed on a small piece of wood to help him forget the sublime pleasures of tobacco. I admired his discipline, especially since he had nothing to do all day long, and smoking a cigarette to idle the time away must have been so tempting. He was very witty and very quick. Once, I found him in the square, his usual haunt, and noticed he didn't have the little stick in the side of his mouth.

"Monsieur Vasquez! Where's your stick?" I asked.

"Oh," he said, with only the barest pause, "the tobacconist is closed."

We would speak Spanish together, mostly. At that time, my Spanish was far better than my French. In fact, what French I knew seemed useless to me; people in the village spoke with such a strong accent —for example, they said *attang* for "wait," instead of *attend*—and I had great trouble comprehending them. So I was happy to speak Spanish in this French village until I could speak and understand this new language capably.

A visit to the Vasquezes' house meant that we would not return home empty-handed. That was impossible. If it wasn't a jar or two of preserved vegetables from their garden, then it might be a rabbit, even, or some leftover *paella,* or some cake, or perhaps some of their illegal, homemade *pastis,* that licorice-tasting apéritif nearly everyone drinks in the south of France. They *rained* things upon us. We tried refusing at first, but gave up because it took too much energy. Later, when Monsieur Vasquez had an operation on his leg and his wife needed rides to the hospital—she couldn't drive a car—we took her. I was glad to be able to give them something in return, at last.

The Vasquezes did not have the best-organized, strictly perfect garden—that honor belonged to Monsieur Noyer—but they had the largest and most chaotic and in many ways the most splendid. It was located, as I mentioned, at the edge of the village, near the little river Darde. I can't begin to tell you everything they grew in it, but it was a catalogue. They also had many fruit trees: apricot, cherry— which we helped them harvest in the spring—fig, apple, more. Oh Lord, I can still taste their cherries now, fat white angels bursting open in my mouth. Madame Vasquez—or Señora Vasquez as I often called her—more than made up for her husband's inability to work. And had no trouble telling me so.

"How's your garden coming along, Señora?" I'd ask.

"*Mucho trabajo.*" Lots of work. She fanned her face with her hand and huffed through her nose.

"Really?"

"Oh, la, la," she said, rolling her eyes, then glancing around to see if anyone else had just arrived. She liked to be apprised of every coming and going in the village, a full-time job. She rode to the garden on her *mobilette,* and it was quite a sight to see her huge body perched on the tiny gray machine, bucket hanging from the handlebar, her enormous skirt discreetly tucked away underneath, her face intent. Some days I'd look out of my window and see her there, in front of our house on her *mobilette,* waving up at me.

"Señor Ricardo! Señor Ricardo!"

"Yes, Señora!" I'd say, poking my head out of a window.

"From the garden!" She held up some lettuce—or whatever. "Take! Take!"

"For us?"

"Si. Si."

And I would bound down the stairs and receive the just-picked gift.

Going to the Vasquezes' garden was always a treat, and it was even better when both of them came along to give us a detailed tour. Theirs was the first garden we ever saw in St. Sébastien, and what an introduction! Both Monsieur and Madame Vasquez had been eager for Iggy and me to see it. It was in late September, only two weeks after we had arrived in the village. The garden was in its waning stages, but we were still bowled over.

Here was row after row after row of just about every vegetable you could think of, each one enormous and hardly able to stand up. Madame Vasquez wandered by this and that, plucking, arranging, tearing.

"Here, string beans," she said. "Here, zucchini. *Mucho trabajo*."

"Those are not zucchini," Monsieur Vasquez said, hobbling along, trying to keep up with us. "Those are eggplant."

Madame Vasquez scowled at him. "Of course

37

they're zucchini!" She clicked her tongue. "Look. Look."

Monsieur Vasquez looked, realized he was wrong, and growled.

"Is this all yours, Señora?" I asked, sweeping my hand to indicate the panorama.

"Yes, all of this. It's too big. Much too big. I must get up every morning at *four o'clock*!" She held up four fingers in front of me.

"Five o'clock," said Monsieur Vasquez.

She frowned. "*Four* o'clock."

He looked away from her, then hobbled over to another plant. She continued walking and surveying.

"Señor Ricardo!" she said. "Look over here. Potatoes! Onions! Beets! Tomatoes!" She reached down, her broad form not seeming to bend, really, but rather to simply lower itself, and ripped a handful of onions from the soft earth. "Take! Take!" She thrust them at me.

I took the onions from her and held them in my fist. Little tough brown whiskers jutted out from the bottom of the bulbs. The skin was sleek and slightly dirty. Their garden seemed to me a paradise, and it seemed to go on forever.

"Eh!" Monsieur Vasquez said. "Over here, Ricardo. Look!"

That's when I got the notion, I'm sure. On that warm September day, down by the river, with the village rising up in the distance, the flaming pink schoolhouse atop it all, the sun washing over us. That's when I got the idea, following this generous Spanish woman down the aisle, as it were, my eyes bugged wide open, as she ripped up an old zucchini plant here, a withered artichoke vine there, shaking the dirt off the old roots, then tossing them aside, that maybe somewhere there was a piece of land here in St. Sébastien de Caisson that I might borrow for the spring and summer. To garden.

SILK

IN OCTOBER, IT RAINED almost every day in St. Sébastien. It rained hard and incessantly, and it left our bones feeling damp. Looking out on the soaked, gray, empty town square, we wondered if the entire year in France was going to be spent indoors. About the middle of the month, our bedroom ceiling began to leak, and we slept with two or three buckets in the room. In the mornings, they were nearly full. For us, the rain was a minor inconvenience, but for others it was far worse. There was a major flood in Nîmes, only twenty minutes away, in which lives were lost. Still, even in the face of a disaster so near,

St. Sébastien remained self-possessed. Aside from one afternoon when old clothes and blankets were collected for the victims, the village remained aloof.

It was difficult in the face of such a constant watery onslaught to get to know more of the people of St. Sébastien de Caisson. Everyone stayed inside. We did, too. We wrote letters, studied French. But I got to know our old stone house very well during that wet October. The house was owned by an American couple. They had restored it over the course of eight years, doing a first-rate job. It was big, cool and solid. It was built of thick, irregularly-shaped gray stones, some the size of fifty-pound blocks of ice, and all held together by wide and narrow tributaries of mortar. It was the first stone house I had lived in, and after twelve months I grew to love its formidable yet friendly massiveness, its slow but sure response to weather, its abidingness. I never thought I would be content living in anything but a wooden house—I lived in a wood-shingle house when I was a boy—but I became a convert and, like many converts, a zealous one. I am now a lover of stone.

Surprisingly, it was also the first *house* in which I had lived with a woman. A New Yorker for so long, I had lived only in apartments. I hadn't foreseen so strong an effect from this. But there it was. I learned that it is very different from sharing an apartment with someone you love, no matter for how long. A house creates bonds an apartment never can. It was wonderful and sometimes difficult for us to share a house. The house was so ample, and we tried to fill it up with love for each other and with generosity for our friends. It didn't always work out that way, as it doesn't always work out that way in many houses elsewhere, but it was particularly sad those times when it didn't work in France, in this little village that we might never see again.

The house had been, as I said, a *magnanerie*, or silkworm nursery, at the time when the cultivation of silkworms was still an important business in the south of France. At the beginning of the nineteenth century, when the house was built—the date 1806 is carved into the stone just above the front door—it was thriving. Evidence of its presence remained. I could see the pockmarks in the exposed roof beams in our bedroom where scores of nails had been driven and from which the silk cocoons once hung, ready to be unraveled by village girls. Narrow stone chimneys had been fabricated into each of the corners of the walls of the bedroom. They led to holes in the roof which, even when we arrived, remained open still. The room, and the silkworms, had been kept warm by the fires that were made on the stone floor in each corner.

Many houses in St. Sébastien were built the same way, and some still had hundreds of thin nails sticking out of the roof beams inside. I often thought about how it must have been so long ago. I would imagine what our bedroom was like at the beginning of the nineteenth century: I pictured a humid, toasty room where hundreds of cocoons dangled by threads. A young peasant woman—perhaps a villager's great-great-grandmother—would come in now and then to check on the worms. I could almost see her, and I could hear her irascible older sister berating her. . . .

"Solange! You nitwit! You've let forty worms die of cold!"

"But . . ."

"You forgot to stoke the fires at dawn."

"Oh, my God."

"God won't help you. You'll be beaten."

Could you hear anything happening, I wondered, in that room full of silkworms? Did they make a noise—a faint hiss?—as they labored away, creating the precious silk thread used to make Madame's dress in Nîmes or Lyon—or even *Paris*? That this house, made of massive, unyielding stone, should have produced something so tenuous as silk thread was a beautiful coincidence I liked to think about from time to time.

The house was furnished with rugged country tables and chairs and had a large kitchen that was a pleasure to cook in. It was supplied with plenty of utensils, including a ponderous black iron pot in which I made the most delicious *provençal* stews I ever hope to make. The stews were delicious because of the things I could put in them, not because of my skills. The tomatoes, garlic and olive oil smelled of the lovely sunlight. A twig of wild thyme, crooked and stunted, added a soft outdoors fragrance of its own. To stimulate the stews, I used an assortment of olives—we had so many levels of appealing bitterness to choose from in France. Everything we bought was superb. The chickens often came with small dossiers attesting to a youth of indolence. They were sprawling and fleshy and, even dead, looked privileged. With all this, if I could just strike a match to light the gas burner under the cast iron pot, I could be a cook of genius.

The casement windows had no screens and threw open to the outside, so we had light. And we had air. Doors were made of heavy wood planks, and they were for the most part wonderfully aged. The floors were new, built of big, smooth, cinnamon tiles. There were even two bathrooms, one for each floor, and the one downstairs had a shower. It was a comfortable place to be, this house, and Iggy made many inventive adjustments—moving things to other rooms and even building a makeshift desk for herself—many of which the owners enthusiastically retained when they returned to claim their house.

It was ideal for guests, too, and we had quite a few, mostly from the Netherlands. They were Dutch friends of Iggy's, pale, polyglot voyagers on their search for the sun. We welcomed them, one and all. We felt proud of the house.

We were trying to learn how to live in France then, to speak and understand the language, to find where to buy things and how much money to spend. We only had a certain amount to last us the entire year, and it wasn't much. Every basic necessity— washing our clothes, for example—seemed to lead us to a new world and at times to an adventure. Iggy was the first to make friends in the village, as she always was whenever we went someplace new. The owners had left us the names and telephone numbers of a few villagers they knew in case we had difficulty. Iggy simply called them. Soon, because of her bold, bright personality, we had our first visitor. And our first dinner guest.

Our first dinner guest was Madame Roque, the short, vociferous, very Gallic-looking widow who was our landlords' best friend in St. Sébastien de Caisson. We were so glad to have her come, but we were very nervous. I'm sure we spent too much money on the meal, buying things we thought would please her. Finally, at precisely eight o'clock, she arrived, calling, "*Ah*-loh! *Ah*-loh!" as she mounted the stairs that led from our *cave,* or basement entry, to the main doorway. I was still in the kitchen, frantically trying to put the meal together. For the main dish, I had made my first rabbit stew. But we shouldn't have worried. She ate like a horse. She ate as if she hadn't eaten in two weeks, finished two helpings, and when she was through, she clacked her false teeth together, snorted through her chronically stopped-up nose, and began telling us stories. The three of us sat around the long wooden table, the dim candlelight glancing dully off the stone walls, Madame Roque talking away, telling us how much she loved *Beel-y Ol-ee-day* and, later, how she was a fervent Communist. "Een America," she said to me, caressing my hands with her cold, waxy fingers as she spoke the few words of English she knew, "mun-ey ees a KEENG!" I looked at Iggy and saw how attentive and comfortable she was. I believe it occurred to both of us at the same moment that this stone house, so wild and strange and old, was finally ours.

WOOD

I MET JULES FAVIER, THE twenty-year-old farmer who was responsible for my having a garden in France, because we had a fireplace.

By late fall, the last warm weather had gone, and, after it had ceased raining, we began waking up to crisp, clean, cool mornings that seemed minted of sun and dew. Even as it grew cooler, the sun's light lost none of its strength. Our bedroom faced east, and I remember waking up one morning in terror because I thought the room was on fire. I blinked my eyes, and I saw it was in fact a large rectangle of yellow, flamelike light from the sun on our stone wall.

I felt foolish, but not that foolish. The sun had that much presence.

By the time it began to grow really cold in St. Sébastien, toward the end of December, what little wood the owners had left us was gone. We wanted a fire every day as well as every evening, *had* to have one. The stone house responded so well to the monstrous fires we made in the quiet nights. The heat rebounded from the thick walls to the couch where Iggy and I sat together, our hands holding glasses of red St. Sébastien wine, our heads bent, eyes dazed by the jumping of the flames.

The end of the wood was a rousing matter. When I asked in the village who had some wood for sale, I was told to talk to Monsieur Valcoze's son, Sully. I wanted to buy wood in St. Sébastien if I could, not from someone outside the village. I didn't know who Sully Valcoze was—it took me almost a year to finally sort out who was who in St. Sébastien, person by person—but that didn't matter. He knew who I was, and soon enough he heard what I wanted.

One brisk, hand-chilling December afternoon, I was outside trying to fix the broken bicycle the owners had left behind. I was wearing my thick leather jacket, I remember, the one I wore during the winter in New York. The village square was empty. I was oblivious in my work. Suddenly, a *mobilette* pulled up abruptly and a man got off quickly and came over to me.

"You want some wood?" he said, not bothering to tell me his name. He was a stocky, smiling man with muscular forearms, unruly hair and runny nose. He wore tight pants, the zipper of which was valiantly trying to remain closed.

"Uh, yes, wood," I said, assuming he must be Sully. He was, of course. Sully Valcoze, thirty-eight years old, bachelor, a sweet man whose only life was his work. Later, he fell so obviously in love with Iggy, but true to his simple soul, he could pursue his passion only by asking me—of all people!—questions about her. "Is Iggy strong?" "Does she like to work outdoors, in the fields?" "Does she get sick often?" "Does she spend a lot of money?" "Can she cook?" Oh, Sully! Now, back in New York, I still wonder where you will ever find your wife.

"You are living here," Sully said to me, "in the Americans' house?" He pointed to our house to make certain I understood.

"Yes," I said, "we're going to be here for a year." I was nervous at this sudden encounter with a villager I'd never met before. What's more, my lips and cheeks were torpid from the cold and unmanageable, and so each word I said in French seemed to acquire an additional consonant or vowel as I literally forced it out of my mouth.

"Ah. Good." He paused and stroked his chin. "And you are from America, too?"

"Yes." We stood facing each other in the cold day.

"Ah. Good." His voice was high and had a whispy timbre, and I found it mesmerizing to listen to.

I took the lead. "Do you have some wood? For sale?"

"Yes," he said. "I have some oak. And I have some *souche*."

"*Souche?* Is that a kind of wood?"

A car sped by us, coming close, not bothering to slow down. The road passed in front of our house, only a few meters from the door.

"No," Sully said, looking at the car briefly. "*Souche* is from the vineyard. It is the best for your fireplace. It burns very, very well." His tone became serious, and he regarded me intently.

"Oh," I said. I didn't know what he meant by *souche*. Later, when he showed me his wood, which was stockpiled in a remote field, I saw that *souche* was simply old vineplants that had been torn up. Sully was right, too: It *was* the best for the fireplace; the twisted, dense, flaky vines burned with a deeply intense fire, producing a face-averting heat.

"How much will you sell the wood for?" I asked.

Sully paused. He stroked his chin again. He glanced away for an instant. "Well," he said earnestly, "if you want the oak, I will have to cut it into small pieces so it can fit in your fireplace. How big is your fireplace?"

"I don't know," I said. Then I spread my arms to try and give an impression.

"Hmm," Sully said, slightly taken aback that I didn't know the measurements, then calculating in his mind. "Cutting wood takes time. It's not easy."

"Yes. Of course," I said sympathetically, not helping my bargaining position.

"So, I would say: 450 francs." That was about seventy dollars. Sully looked at me cautiously. "But that will be enough wood to keep you warm for the winter."

"And you would bring it here, next to the house?"

"*Bien sûr,*" Sully said, his wood-spiced voice rising. Of course.

I thanked him and said I'd think about it. He shrugged his shoulders, smiled, quickly got back on his *mobilette* and left as abruptly as he had arrived. His frame was ramrod straight on the seat as the little machine sped off. He seemed in a hurry. Later I realized he always seemed in a hurry.

I went back inside to talk to Iggy about all of this.

Now, by this time, near the beginning of January, we had lived in St. Sébastien de Caisson for nearly four months, and I felt something was missing. We weren't *connecting* with the village as much as I had hoped. The villagers themselves were cordial, but not forthcoming, and even Iggy's readiness to engage people in talk wasn't enough. In most cases, for some reason—maybe because there had been just too many transient renters here before us—one thing did not lead to another. Except for the handful of friends we had made, like Monsieur and Madame Vasquez, St. Sébastien more or less ignored us. Actually, the Vasquezes were themselves somewhat isolated, maybe because they were Spanish. We felt frustrated. And we felt lonely.

I was not going to spend a year in France this way. I was not going to leave this village in a state of ignorance, not having *delved* into the life they led—not having met them, talked with them, drunk with them, laughed with them. I didn't care how closed a society they were. *But how to break through?* Gentility, courtesy and cordialness obviously were not enough. I used to ponder this problem like a detective as I sat in the second-floor room I used as my studio, and where I wrote. Every once in a while, I'd get up from my desk and look out the window at daily life that was unfolding down below in the square. I could see it all, a sweeping view. I'd see all the men and women I didn't know and wonder what they were like. That man there, on the tractor, who *was* he?

This wood problem—coupled with our continuing concern about money—gave me an idea, though.

A few days after my conversation with Sully, I spotted him on his *mobilette,* and I waved him to a stop. I made a simple suggestion to him. Simple, but . . . He would deliver enough wood to us to last us the winter. And I would pay for the wood with my labor. *Yes,* I would work for him—in the fields, around his house, it didn't matter. Sully looked genuinely surprised. His head moved backward an inch or two, and his eyes widened.

"Work?" he said. "But you're an American. You don't have to work."

"Uh, well," I said, amused and amazed at this caricature of the rich American, "actually, some of us do work—occasionally." I could see, though, how the life we led in the village might add fuel to his preconception; we didn't *do* much—on the surface, anyway—did we? My work was inside, not a proper job outdoors, like theirs.

"Ah. Good," Sully said in response to my protest. But I wasn't sure he believed me.

"I'll do any kind of work," I said, holding up my hands in readiness. "Even though I'm an American"—I smiled at him—"I *do* know how to work. Really."

"Well," he said, "I don't know. I will have to talk with my father and my brother."

"So—there's a possibility?"

"I don't know," Sully said. "I can't promise anything. I will have to talk to them."

"All right," I said. I shook his large, rough hand warmly—I wanted to instill a sense of foregone conclusion into this encounter—and we parted. He sped away on his *mobilette,* his head glancing from side to side, looking, his body wonderfully straight. I had no idea what would happen, but I was proud of myself for the attempt.

When I told Iggy about what had happened, she was excited.

"What a great idea," she said. "Do you think he'll actually give you some work?"

"I don't know. He didn't give me a *clue,* not a hint either way."

"What's he like?"

"Seemed a very nice guy. But in a hurry."

I wondered. And I waited.

Three days later, Monsieur Valcoze—not Sully, but his father—came to the door of our *cave,* and knocked loudly.

"Can you be in the field tomorrow morning at seven-thirty?" He shoved his beret back slightly with his hand and scratched his forehead.

"Certainly. Of course," I said.

"Good," he said.

"But . . . where? What field?" I asked.

"Ah. Good. Sully will come here tomorrow morning on his *mobilette.* You can follow him."

"Oh, that's good," I said. Everything I said sounded stupid.

"Well," he said, "until tomorrow."

"Yes, tomorrow," I said. He turned and walked away. "And thank you!" I said to him as he ambled off. He waved a hand at me without looking back.

I took a breath. I'd done it! I'd gotten work! We would have our wood, and I would pay for it by working for the Valcozes. From this minute on, I was sure our lives in St. Sébastien were going to change. That's all they did, the villagers, work. Now, I would, too. Like them. I couldn't help but imagine what conversations the father and two brothers had had about me and my questionable American stamina.

"You want to hire an American? Why, you might as well just give him the wood, free."

"Who knows? Maybe he *can* work."

"Have you ever seen an American work?"

"Well . . ."

 STONES

IT WAS A CHILL DAY, and the sun had not yet risen, but even so the large square was active. Tractors entered, headlights guiding them across the sea of space, driven by hunched figures obscured in the darkness; people got into their cars hurriedly, started them up and drove quickly away; *mobilettes* whizzed by. The air was remarkably fresh and cool. I wish I could give you a taste of it now. How sharp and subtle it was, with the faintest odor of the vineyards, a clean, earthy air, and distinctly French somehow. As the darkness faded, I could see the villagers take quick, curious glances at me as they went off to work. Standing there in the new morning, I felt the same small panic I felt when I was sixteen and went to work at construction in Virginia for older men I didn't know. I had gotten myself into this. Now, what?

At exactly seven-thirty, Sully sped up to the house on his *mobilette*. He halted, placed one leg on the ground and let the engine continue sputtering.

"Good day," he said smiling. "Are you ready?" He was dressed in exactly the same clothes as before.

"Yes," I said. "I'm ready." I doubt if that was true. Sully nodded and turned to go.

I got into my Peugeot 104 and started it up to follow Sully as he began to drive away. As I wheeled the car around, trying to keep an eye on Sully's accelerating *mobilette,* I heard a familiar voice shout, "Hey!" I slowed down a bit, looked back, and I saw Iggy leaning out of the second-story window, grasping her bathrobe to her neck against the cold, waving a huge hand at me and shouting, for all the world to hear, in French, "Good luck! Work hard!" I leaned my head out of the car window and waved back at her. Then I turned back and picked up speed. As Sully and I descended the little road that led away from the village, and the house became smaller and smaller, I watched Iggy in my rearview mirror, her diminishing figure waving, waving, waving.

Just past the edge of the village, where a rectangular sign with black letters declared, ST. SÉBASTIEN

DE CAISSON, Sully banked down a narrow road which led into the vineyards. I followed. Into the vineyards! Into the heart and soul of what possessed the villagers, of what was their *life*. By now, the leaves had fallen off all the trees, so we drove past rows and rows of skeletal vineplants. The sense of fecundity we saw when we first arrived was gone now; what remained was the hopelessness of winter. The vineplants looked even more deathly in the demi-light. Sully kept on a while longer, then turned abruptly down a dirt path. Even in the naked cold, his posture remained perfectly straight. We continued a bit further until we reached a small gathering of cars and men at the edge of a large, cleared field. Sully stopped and got off. This field looked odd, devoid as it was of vineplants; it was an *empty* field.

As I pulled my car to a stop, I could see Monsieur Valcoze and three other men I didn't know. A tractor was already moving in the field, digging out lengthy trenches. Later, I learned that the driver was Sully's older brother, Raymond-Charles. Monsieur Valcoze approached my car curiously, his eyes squinting in inquiry.

"Ah! The American!" he said, finally recognizing me. "How are you?" He had on his beret, his battered pants, his old cardigan and his plaid shirt buttoned up to his throat. He hadn't shaved.

I shook his hand. "Please—call me Richard."

"Richard?" he said, taking a small step backward in mock wonderment. "Richard the Lion-Hearted?"

"Well . . ."

"Come this way," he said, ignoring my response. At times when he spoke, I had great difficulty understanding him; his words always seemed particularly hard to discern, adding to my sense of insecurity. But this time he beckoned me with a hand, and so I understood.

"Today," he said, turning to me as we walked, "we will *défoncer*."

"Oh?" I said. "Good."

I had no idea what he meant.

We reached the group of men. I looked at them all quickly, nodded and mumbled, *"Bonjour,"* but I was too stimulated to take them in. Sully came up to me. He pointed to the tractor, which was scooping up the earth with its sleek, curved blade, making parallel trenches the length of the field.

"We will follow in the trench on foot and take out any rocks and old roots we find," he said.

"Ah. Good," I said, unconsciously speaking like him. So *this* was the work. Much later, I understood that the new vineplants would be planted in this field, and that it had to be cleared of any underground obstructions to let the young roots grow freely deep into the earth.

I followed Sully and the other men across the field,

negotiating the soft earth, until we reached the first trench. We all hopped down into the same trench, and everyone spread out, covering the length. It was about shoulder deep. From a distance, an observer, unaware of the depression, might see heads bobbing along just above ground level. The earth was cool and humid in the trench and very uneven, so traversing it was not easy. I could smell the dampness. It was a clayey earth I would come to know well in the following months.

The sun began to rise. I saw the orange coin suspended above St. Sébastien in the distance. It was a welcome sight in the chill air. The village looked old and beautiful.

I decided to stay close to Sully, following his example. He walked down his section of the trench, and whenever he spotted a stone or an old vine root, he bent and picked it up and tossed it on the ground above him next to the trench. The roots were often rangy and reluctant, still clutching the earth. Eventually, a truck would come and take all the piled stones and roots away. Sully worked very fast. I began to do the same thing. As I walked forward, I sometimes lost my balance in the disrupted ground, and I had to slap my hand against the sticky side for support. The stones the tractor unearthed were gray, sandy and cold. They were of varying sizes. Most, though heavy, and not always easy to dislodge, I could lift myself. Some, however, were too big, and I needed Sully's muscle to help to lift, then push, them up over the side of the trench. *"Un. Deux. TROIS,"* we'd say and push ourselves into the lifting. Sometimes we were literally shoulder to shoulder, hands sliding from place to place on the cold, sandy surface, searching for a sure spot to hold on. We did not want the large rock to slide from our grasp and fall back onto our feet, a distinct possibility. I put every ounce of American strength I had into the job. Sully and I were battling in the trenches together then, comrades in arms, and I wanted to do my share.

I followed behind the tractor closely as it made its way up and down the field. When the blade unfolded the earth, sometimes it struck directly a large stone, steel grinding against rock and wet dirt, sparks shooting off—sometimes so close they glanced off my pants. Some rocks were just too great even for the tractor and, despite Raymond-Charles's adroit and creative manipulation of the powerful blade, those had to be left where they were. I wondered if this would inhibit the growth of the new plants, but Sully said no. I began to find a rhythm, doing my work at nearly the same speed as the tractor's progress. On and on I went.

This was *labor*.

From time to time, I would check to see if I was working as hard as the others. It seemed to me that I was, but of course I was never certain. I was beginning to get tired, I knew that. My back was speaking to me. At one point, after I'd been working a good while, Sully walked over to me and smiled.

"I can believe my eyes now," he said in his woody voice. "Because I can see that an American can work."

I stood up, the hot sweat pouring down my neck, the cold air hovering around me. I smiled. The praise soared through my body. He really *was* a sweet man, Sully, so free of competitiveness and guile. As I looked at him, at his hair that grew crazily in all directions, I could see, on the corner of his mouth, the yellow of egg yolk jutting out from his smile. At that moment I felt extraordinarily grateful for his praise; it felt sublime. And I couldn't resist pressing him:

"It's really true?"

"*Bien sûr,*" he said.

About eleven o'clock, we paused to rest a few minutes by Monsieur Valcoze's ancient white station wagon and to have something to drink. I met Raymond-Charles, who drove the tractor and whom I would in time come to see as so unlike his brother. I met Julien, another smiling St. Sébastiener who, I eventually found out, was married to Monsieur and Madame Vasquez's daughter. I met a taciturn Moroccan named Ahmed.

And I met Jules.

 JULES

I DON'T RECALL if I had any dramatic first impressions of the young farmer who would play so large a part in our lives in St. Sébastien, but I do know now that meeting him that day was the most auspicious thing that happened to us that year in the south of France. What a stroke of luck that we ran out of firewood, that we were a bit low on cash, that we felt so alone in this place!

There was something immediately appealing about Jules. He was a tall, lanky man—a *man,* despite his twenty-few-years—with sinewy forearms and large hands, both powerful. I can see him even now, as he leaned against Monsieur Valcoze's car, dressed in just a sleeveless sweatshirt against the cold, muscles working as he took a drink. He had sharp, narrow eyes, high rough cheekbones and sensuous lips. His dark hair was slightly disheveled from working in the open air. He had the seasoned face of a *paysan,* a man who had worked the land perhaps ten years already. His mien was mostly serious.

As things developed, it was because of this strong, highly opinionated, most loyal French farmer that I had a garden in France—though, in fact, gardening interested him hardly at all.

In addition to his considerable strength, of which he was both certain and proud, and notwithstanding that he could at times be as frivolous and wild as any of the young villagers, he had, I was to see, an exacting intelligence. He tended to point out sternly the most minute error in my French, and he could be quite disapproving if I made the same mistake twice. Eventually, I was to call Jules *"mon professeur."* And so it was appropriate that our first conversation there by Monsieur Valcoze's battered field car in the French winter day, amongst men taking slow drinks of water, should be about vocabulary. Language has always been an easy way for me to approach a new situation, and so I said,

"Could you help me, please?"

"Ah. Good," he said a bit surpised, even though he'd surely seen me looking at him.

"I'm trying to learn the words, the French words, for things," I said, approaching him. "For example, what we're doing today, here, in the fields, it's called *défoncer?*"

"Yes." He looked as if he expected more.

"What *exactly* does that mean?"

"*Bon,*" he said calmly. Then he went on to carefully tell me, pointing at the field where we had worked, that the word *défoncer* meant to dig a trench; obviously in St. Sébastien it also took on the meaning to clear rocks and roots. But the word also could mean to *knock in,* as in a policeman coming to your house and, not gaining entry, *défoncer* your door.

"*Tu as bien compris?*" he said, looking at me doubtfully. You really have understood?

"Yes, yes," I said. "Really. By the way, I'm Richard. The American."

"I am Jules Favier," he said, and we shook hands. "From St. Sébastien de Caisson." He smiled slightly at this.

After the break, we went back to the trench together and worked side by side the rest of the morning until it was time to stop for lunch. He was working for Monsieur Valcoze as a favor. Another time, when his family needed a hand in the fields, Sully or Raymond-Charles would come and help them. As we pulled and pushed, I asked him word after word for the things I didn't know about what we were doing. I learned wonderful words from him that day. Words like *argile* (clay); *argileux* (clayey); *gel* (frost); *arracher* (to pull up or out, uproot—which is what they did to the old vineplants to clear the field); *ronger* (to gnaw, nibble—which is what the frost does to the rocks); *désagréger* (to break up—which is what the cold, at its most severe, would do to the rocks); and more. Difficult words for my poor American mouth to say correctly in the cold French air! Jules had to repeat them often, correcting my imprecisions carefully. As I struggled to say and retain these words, it was plain to me that language was important to Jules. These words gave a kind of meaning to his life. In a sense, they were almost as important to him, a farmer, as the weather.

We stopped exactly at noon. I was glad. It had been a long morning. My nervous energy was gone, and I was tired. Toward the end, I had to push myself. Muscles I hadn't used in years had to be forced, at mental gunpoint, to go on. I felt I had acquitted myself well, though. Both Sully and Monsieur Valcoze came over and thanked me as I walked to my car. Monsieur Valcoze looked at me expectantly.

"You will return after lunch, Richard?"

"Yes, yes," I said. "*Bien sûr.*"

"*Bon,*" he said and walked off to his car.

I said goodbye to Jules, and I said I would like to talk with him again. "I mean in the village," I said, "after we're done working in the fields."

"Yes," he said straightforwardly. "When I finish

my work, I am always in the village, by the school. I am not so difficult to find."

"*Dés-a-gra-ger?*" I asked him one more time.

"*Dés-a-GRÉ-ger,*" he said, emphasizing the third syllable.

I got in my car and drove back through the fields to the village and our house. What a morning! But how was I going to last the afternoon? All the strength in my arms was gone, and they hung limply down the sides of my body like an orangutan's. I trudged upstairs and went inside. There Iggy, who had seen my car approach from the window, was waiting for me with a cup of hot chocolate.

I took it eagerly. I still felt the aura of damp earth and cold swirling about me. I took a slow, healing sip.

"Well," she said, sitting down next to me, studying my jeans and shirt caked with dirt and my frigid outdoors face, "how was it?"

"Great," I said. "I'll tell you all about it. But guess what?" She edged closer to me. I smiled at her. "I think maybe we have a new friend."

 MON AMI

THE SCHOOL, WHICH WAS PINK, was next to our house, and I used to watch the children gather and play in the morning before the schoolmistress came outside and clapped her hands to force them all inside. Later in the day, around five o'clock, after school was over and the children had gone home, cars would begin to pull up right onto the flat, granulated yard in front of the school. Various young St. Sébastieners would emerge from their Peugeots and Renaults to pass an hour or two talking, joking and listening to their car radios or cassette players. The music was always played loudly, and car doors were left open to let the sound explode into the far corners of St. Sébastien. It was so loud sometimes that I swear pencils left on our dining room table shuddered. I was always impressed at how much these friends had to say to one another. Most of them worked in the fields all day, so what news did they have to report? But the talk was continuous and even competitive.

Jules was always a part of this group. He drove a bright blue Renault 12, and so it was easy to spot him. And I *was* looking for him. I was looking for a chance to pursue that preliminary warm meeting in the fields. I had forced myself to return to *défoncer* that first afternoon, so Sully and Monsieur Valcoze and Julien now said hello to me and knew my name, but I had the feeling Jules was my chance at something deeper. I might have been mistaken, but I thought *he* had begun glancing over our way to look for *me*. Our house was one of the largest in St. Sébastien, and it must have been a bit mysterious to everyone. It was natural that the young people in the schoolyard would look over reflexively at the house from time to time, especially since they knew two foreigners were going to be living there for an entire year. But I had the definite sense Jules was looking for me.

One winter afternoon, I thought I'd waited long enough, and I simply went over to the afternoon group and said hello. They were all polite, but reticent. Jules, however, made a little conversation, for which I was grateful. I invited him to come over for a *pastis* and to meet Iggy. He didn't seem to like that idea. He looked down, mumbled, and moved the pebbly ground with his foot.

"Please," I said, "come over to the house. Iggy very much wants to meet you."

He looked up. *"Bon,"* he said simply. Good. He followed me to the house, glancing back at the others with a reluctant look, as if his music teacher had just come to fetch him to practice.

This reluctance was, I would come to see, characteristic of Jules. He did not feel comfortable accepting—invitations, gifts, help. In that, he was somewhat like his father. But once you broke through, and he took, he was often childlike in his pleasure at what he had been given. No matter how doleful he looked that winter day, I was glad I urged him on. Because at last in St. Sébastien de Caisson, one thing *did* lead to another. Jules walked cautiously into the house and, like a servant invited into the dress ball for a midnight toast, chose the most unobtrusive way to conduct his visit, remaining standing until we forced him to sit, refusing something to drink until we compelled him to take *something,* leaving at the first acceptable moment. But after that first visit, he came again. And again. He became accustomed to the idea of his presence in our house. Iggy, who was nervy and completely unintimidated by this laconic *paysan,* brought Jules out like a flower. She teased him gently, and though at times he huffed at her, it was easy to see that he liked her.

"Jules," she might say to him, "why don't you have a girlfriend?"

"How do you know I don't?"

"Oh, I know. I also know Véronique likes you a lot." Véronique was a village girl who was madly in love with Jules. This week.

"Véronique?" He would snort. "She's only sixteen. Too young!"

"And you?" Iggy would say. "My old man of twenty. Come here, let me see all your gray hair!"

"Stay away from me you . . . Dutch woman!"

"Hey! Don't say any bad things about my country!"

"Bah."

Though he was intensely loyal and generous, he could be haughty and cold, sometimes scolding me. We were at times frustrated by the other's behavior. And with Jules Favier, there will always be something that will remain private. Secret, even. Part of this is because he is a French farmer from a very small, insular village. Part of it is simply because he is Jules.

He was very cooperative when it came to answering my many questions about the land, providing me with detailed responses. In one of my notebooks I still have a list of all the varieties of grapes (fifteen) grown in St. Sébastien. It is written in Jules's formal, slightly quavery hand. Sometimes, though, when I asked him a question, he would blink in slight astonishment at the sheer obviousness of the answer. I had asked about something—I never knew what question would make him react this way—that should be given knowledge for anybody—even for an American.

"Listen, Jules!" I would say, bristling to see that incredulous look on his face. "I'm from New York. We don't have vineyards there. I just don't *know* these things!"

"Evidently," he would say.

Mon professeur. Yes, my teacher, always correcting my French—even today, still, in his letters: "*Pas quitter de fumer, mais* arrêter *de fumer.*" My pronunciation, too, was expected to be perfect. "In French," he would tell me solemnly, "in this case you do not pronounce the last letter. You do not speak good French if you do." Yes, Professor.

My relationship with him, begun that day heaving stones in the fields, was to be made fast by the travails of my garden. I'm not sure what he ultimately thought of me as a gardener, but I do know that he felt, as did all St. Sébastieners who had a vineyard and worked it, that once a job was begun it must be done as it should be done.

Through him, I met his brothers, Eugène, Thierry and Paul, all of them as surprisingly different as only brothers can be. I met his parents, Gilbert and Marie-Rose, who were delightful and who put up with my garden problems, which so often stole their son away from his legitimate labor. And I met his grandfather, Georges, and his grandmother, Lucette. Meeting them, I felt I'd entered the nineteenth century. They were the earth, and their faces and bodies showed it. Georges, slow, bent, tough, would often say, "*Ma foi.*" My faith, a phrase I'd only seen in books.

Even the tragedy that touched them seemed to come from a bygone era.

In poring through the records in the town hall, I came upon information about the villagers living in contemporary St. Sébastien. And one day I saw recorded the deaths of two children of Georges and Lucette Favier, two boys who had died in the late 1940s, aged two and four. I remember staring at the names. Had they lived, they would have been about my age today. I had learned something about Georges and Lucette without their knowledge, and I felt a bit like an intruder. But I was also fascinated. It struck me as I looked at the straightforward representation of great loss, that these children would be buried in the little cemetery at the edge of the village. I had been there before. I went to the cemetery occasionally to lift my spirits, strange as that may sound. It was walled, as in most small French towns, and the wall was made of a soothing gray stone. Inside, it was green, well tended, and the only place where cypress trees grew. I liked to stand and watch those tall trees sway slightly in the breeze.

The next day I walked down to the cemetery and looked from grave to grave, searching. I found the boys, side by side. They each had a small tombstone, their first names printed large: Favier, LOUIS and Favier, JEAN-MARIE. Dead. How, I never knew. I imagined scarlet fever. Much later, when I asked Jules, he did not know and had only a vague knowledge of his lost uncles. I stayed a while by their graves, then I walked home thinking that it would not be such a bad place to rest forever, this little green place, with the cypresses to watch over me.

Four or five months later, Iggy and I were having dinner at Georges and Lucette's. Lucette was telling us where all her children lived, and what they did. She went through the list one by one, remembering the names and counting them off on her fingers. When she reached the last one, her youngest daughter, she said,

"And . . . Jacqueline. Yes. That makes six." She smiled. Then she paused, looked slightly away at no one in particular, and said, very softly, "We were eight once."

I don't know why Jules consented to let me work with him. Or why he chose for me the job of pruning the vineplants in the spring. But I suspect, knowing

Jules, this was a kind of gift. Though I had begged him to give me work, pruning was something different. It was an exact, delicate job, a life-and-death matter, in which some shoots were sliced off, while others were left to live. The tool was a pair of sharp pruning shears which had to be held with two hands. I did the best I could, but I was no *paysan,* and this was more than simple physical labor. I made mistakes. When I sliced deep into the tough living arm of a shoot that should have been left to grow, I killed an important being. It had blood—what was sap, anyway?—it produced offspring, and, as Sully had told me, it would live about as long as I would.

At those times, seeing what I had done, I'd let out a deep groan. Jules would approach me, look at the dangling shoot, and calmly tell me, "That's all right. But be more careful next time." I was grateful, but I disliked doing less than an adequate job; and I disliked even more taking money for it. But evidently I was not completely disastrous, because I pruned with Jules more than once. When *he* pruned, he was graceful, sure and exact. He would edge his scissors carefully into a nook of the vineplant; the little jaws of the shears would open, and he would squeeze them carefully around the small shoot he wanted removed, which was perilously close to one he didn't want touched.

"You've got to be a surgeon," he'd say as the steel blades, shaped like an eagle's beak, crisply pinched off the branch, leaving the neighbor unmolested. *That* was farming.

Walking down a vineyard, down a strict lane of vineplants on a cool spring day, cutting with great concentration, trying to make the correct decisions in rapid style—Jules, his scissors turning and darting within the branches, pruned two plants for every one of mine—I was struck by the sheer joy of responsibility. We were always completely alone in the big quiet vineyard, and the only noise you could hear was the *snap, snap, snap* of the shears. It was just us, working in the blue vault of the French day. And Jules had made me a part of it all.

 BLOOMING

"Intimacy with another country," Shirley Hazzard has said, "is nurtured through long wet winters as well as radiant days." Our winter in St. Sébastien wasn't particularly wet, but it was long. The February nights were black and cold. Sometimes they seemed endless. Fortunately, we had the big hearth and lots of *souche,* and so we had a fire most of the time to warm and cheer us. We kept the fire in the daytime, too, and that saved us money since we didn't have to use as much of our heating oil. On a winter morning, Iggy loved to come downstairs in her robe with a cup of tea and luxuriously wake up sitting on the big couch by the fire. It was lovely, too, to have lunch with a fire going and hear the hiss and snap of the wood, feel the aura of warmth, a countermeasure to the cold day. After five o'clock, when the sun went down, the village pretty much withdrew into itself, and we were left to ourselves, all alone in our big stone house until the sun rose thirteen or fourteen hours later.

The dictionary says winter is "the cold season between autumn and spring." True. Between two robust periods of the year—one revealing its beauty in the agony of death, the other in the agony of birth—is the dead season, as Villon says. In this small village, where it snows only once every two or three years, the feeling of winter's emptiness was enhanced by the plain stone houses, the echoing square and the absence of a warm, friendly café busy with talk and cups raised to lips. Winter was a time when it was easier for me to miss my brother and sister and their children, when I grew tired of expressing myself in French, when I yearned to have a visitor from my own country. I was feeling a bit melancholy, and my writing didn't seem to be going as well as I had hoped. Iggy found diversion and purpose in a local choral group, and she used to go every Tuesday evening to practice in a nearby village. She made new friends among the amateur singers and often came home alive with inspiration, waving a score by

Rossini or Mozart and singing her favorite passages for me.

The compensations of a restive winter in St. Sébastien, however, were memorable. We often took late evening walks into the cold night. For one thing, this prevented us from going to bed too early, which in the winter we always wanted to do. Oh, just to crawl under those sweet, heavy blankets! We would put on our coats and gloves and scarves and walk out into the chill black night for twenty or thirty minutes. The sky was exactly like those maps of stars you see with the lines connecting one to the other, insouciantly linking billions of miles, to form the shape of a warrior or bear or some other constellation. They were *all* there. Even on a preternaturally clear midnight in Wyoming, I have never seen such a commonwealth of stars. I am not a lover of stars. I think I find them too disturbingly incomprehensible. I prefer the moon. But on those hand-held, or glove-held, walks down the road that led past the schoolyard, I could look at the population of stars without worrying so much.

We also took walks in the Cévennes Mountains. Those beautiful hills—for they aren't really quite mountains—Robert Louis Stevenson describes so well in his little book, *Travels with a Donkey*, became our favorite place in France. The Cévennes are as profound as they are delightful. They were refuge to both the Camisards and the Maquisards. The former were resistance fighters against the state-imposed Catholicism in the late seventeenth century and the latter against German-imposed fascism in the twentieth. I felt the Cévennes held many secrets, and it made me feel good to be in the presence of such wise earth. We would take long walks in those stony old hills, even in the middle of winter. I can still hear the dull sound of goats' bells clanking in the frosty air, coming from someplace I couldn't determine. The Cévennes helped make my winter uneasiness tolerable. But still I was biding my time, until spring.

If you live in a northern climate, it can be difficult to determine exactly when spring begins. If you live in New York, you may never know. But in St. Sébastien de Caisson, I saw spring arrive with the clarity and brightness of a trumpet call. It all took place on two acres of land not far from our house.

Down at the foot of the village, past the schoolhouse but before the *cave coopérative,* was an orchard of apricot trees. There were many, many trees lined up one after the other, all perfectly straight. They were owned by St. Sébastien's richest man, Monsieur Pallot. Monsieur Pallot was a bulky, olive-skinned man who lived at the top of the village in a grand house with St. Sébastien's only swimming pool. Besides the orchard, he owned two garden stores in Alès. He had two children: a boy of twelve, who was beginning to look as ample as his father; and a daughter, a most exquisite little girl with a Nefertiti-like profile. Even at nine years old, she had the pouty arrogance of her station. Though I found her superior regard annoying, I couldn't keep my eyes off her. She was marvelous. On her infrequent weekends home from boarding school, she floated through the village, an imperial presence with perfect skin and brown eyes. By then, I felt a bit like a villager myself, basic and plain, and I shrank from her, like a rustic before a Lady.

Jules's family had apricot trees, too, but not as many as Monsieur Pallot. I don't know how many Monsieur Pallot had, but surely over one hundred. A French apricot tree grows to be roughly twelve to fifteen feet high, with many slim, outspreading branches. In the winter, like everything else, the branches on the trees were bare. In February, though, buds appeared along the entire length of each branch, and in early March, they began to bloom. (I discovered that the word *apricot* comes from the Latin word *praecoquum,* meaning "to ripen early.") I don't remember the exact day when I realized what was happening at the foot of the hill, but I know for me that was the day winter ended.

I had never seen apricot blossoms before. Scores of pinkish-yellow buds detonated on each branch, and scores of trees were in bloom, each with hundreds of blossoms on them. The color was overwhelming. I walked down to the orchard and wandered into this affluence. I reached up and touched the flowers. They were as soft-hued and frail as Japanese rice paper. Winter had been soundly defeated by the most delicate vanquisher. Moreover, the blossoms had a scent—they smelled slightly of apricots, but floral as well. The smell of apricots in March! The familiar estival tang! I went from blossom to blossom, nosing in the scent like a bee, a 170-pound bee.

And I knew exactly what I was going to do.

THE GARDEN

 LAND

"YOU WANT A PIECE OF LAND? To have a garden?" Jules Favier asked me incredulously. "Why? You can have all the vegetables you want, free, from my grandfather's garden."

"But I want my *own* land, to raise my *own* vegetables," I said.

"You're crazy," Jules said; his vehemence seemed a matter of pride.

"Maybe," I said and smiled at Jules. "Anyway, that's what I want. Can you help me?" Yes, that's what I wanted. That's what I had decided that early

March day by Monsieur Pallot's sensational apricot trees. And I was going to have it; I felt it in my heart.

"You Americans are . . ." He whirled his finger next to his head.

"Yes. Yes. But *can* you help me?"

It was April. We stood in front of the door of our house opposite the town hall of St. Sébastien de Caisson. It was a damp, gloomy day, and both of us shifted about on the gravel to keep warm. Now and then a car would pass through the town square on its way to another village, and Jules would turn and regard it with an animal-like intensity as it went by.

"Well?" I pressed.

"I don't know. Let me think." He looked down at the ground, as was his custom when he was not ready to make a decision. It was late afternoon. No one else was about. The dull spring light made the stone village, already a monotony of gray, even more somber. In the distance I could see a tractor moving languidly through a vineyard. Down the way, an old woman peeked her head out of her door and withdrew it after a few seconds. Just then Jules's older brother Thierry drove up in his car. These kinds of spontaneous encounters were always occurring in the village. Meetings and partings were an essential fabric of village life.

Thierry got out and came over to us. He was slightly shorter than Jules and thinner, but he was handsomer, with an open, seductive smile. He was indeed the oldest brother, and he was more serious than the other Favier brothers, watchful, with the extra burden of responsibility the first sibling inherits as a birthright. As always, he shook hands with me. Briefly, Jules explained the situation to him. Thierry stroked his chin slowly, bowed his head, pondered. After a few minutes, he spoke directly to Jules.

"What about that corner next to the old vineyard? In back of Polge's land?"

"Could be," he said.

"There's a stream nearby," Thierry said. "Down below."

Jules added, "It's away from the road. So people won't be able to see."

"Or take anything," Thierry finished.

"You mean," I said eagerly, "*you* might have a piece of land for me—that I could borrow or rent?"

"I don't know," Jules said. He sniffled, then looked up sharply. He searched the distance, relaxed, a false alarm.

"But!" I said.

"Might be," Jules said. "I'll have to ask my father. It's his land. But normally, with something like this, I don't think he will have a problem."

"I want to pay you. You know, something for the rent of the land." I was getting very excited. "I don't know how much money to offer, but . . ."

He cut me off. "It's not a question of money. If

my father says it's all right, then you don't need to pay him."

"Unbelievable!" I said in English. Then back to French, "My own garden."

Thierry and Jules looked at one another. Thierry smiled his wonderful, open smile. Jules gave me his characteristic disapproving look.

"Americans," he snorted. But I could tell he was pleased.

Just then there was Albin Polge, the barrel-chested, jocular, myopic mayor of St. Sébastien, on his way across the square from the town hall to his home. He waved a greeting at us, lowered his head and passed on along.

"Ah, Jules," I said to him as he watched the mayor turning a corner, "could you take me to see the piece of land?"

Jules was still concentrating on the point where the mayor had disappeared around the corner. "Naturally," he said, a bit vaguely.

"Now?"

"*Now?*" He turned and looked at me. I nodded insanely. He paused, then looked over to Thierry. The two brothers exchanged a brief, unspoken communication. Thierry shrugged his shoulders slightly. Jules looked down; he was thinking.

"Well," he said, "perhaps we can go now. If you want."

"Fantastic!" I said.

"We will go in my car," Jules said.

The three of us walked over to Jules's blue Renault
12. It was a classic European sedan, small, taut, effi-
cient. He was very proud of it, and he spent most
of his free time either riding in it or improving it
in some way. We got in. Jules put on an Eagles
tape as usual, turned the volume up very high, and
we sped off at a terrifying clip. Jules thought himself an excellent driver. He gripped the wheel with
two hands, and, in fact, drove like a professional:
intensely, calmly and very fast. I loved to ride in
his car.

We drove first past the pink schoolhouse where
Jules had gone to school and where his father had,
too. And where his sons would someday probably
go, too. Then we drove past Monsieur Pallot's stately
apricot trees, naked once again, and past Monsieur
Armand's one-hundred-year-old olive oil mill. We
drove out of the village, down my favorite French
road.

The atmosphere was astonishingly clear, as always.
Even though it was a gray, cloudy day, I could see
everything extraordinarily well. I could see figures
moving, almost imperceptibly, in distant fields, and
even though they were at least a mile away, the light
made everything so distinct that I could make a good
guess as to who they were.

I looked ahead of me down the little road as we
sped along, and savored my anticipation.

About two kilometers from St. Sébastien, in the middle of nowhere, Jules slowed down.

"Are we here?" I said, trying to be heard above the music.

He didn't answer. Instead, he pulled the car over and turned down a small lane next to a vineyard. About fifty meters from the road, he stopped.

"Well," he looked at me, "here it is."

I turned all around. There was nothing but the long, still monotonous vineplants. "Uh, where, Jules?" I said.

He smiled. It amused him when he knew something I didn't. "Come on," he directed.

We got out, and he led me to a bank. Down below was a small stream. So, there was water nearby. *That* was good. We descended and slogged through the shallow, muddy water and over to a small rise about twenty meters away. We negotiated this uneasily, our feet sliding away from under us because of the mud we had picked up crossing the stream. We finally made it and emerged onto a small, unevenly-shaped plateau.

Was this it? The small plot of land, about the size of a suburban driveway, was infested with weeds and bushes. On two sides, it was bordered by a vineyard. The other two sides by thick, unruly briers with daggerlike thorns. I could hear the stream somewhere nearby. I took a breath. Up above, the sky was completely open. No big trees blocked the sun, or what would be the sun when the clouds went away. I bent down and touched the ground. In my excitement, I lost all sense of place, and time. Suddenly, there was a deep stirring within me. I looked at Jules and Thierry, both of whom were staring at the land intently, taking in every detail with their ever-searching eyes.

"Here," said Jules without ceremony. "Here, you can make your garden."

 PLANTING

I DON'T THINK IT'S so easy to make a garden too small, but it's very easy to make a garden too big. This I did, and magnificently. After Jules had come with his tractor and cleared the land, ripping the earth apart and revealing all its lusciousness, I began to think about what to plant. There was still lots of work to be done—the raking and harrowing—before I could actually put the seeds and plants into the ground, but nevertheless I felt I could begin to make some decisions. I avoided any barrier to my garden fantasies with the simple solution of not excluding anything. "Everything is permitted, nothing is forbidden." That was the motto of my garden in St. Sébastien de Caisson.

Like Noah, I denied no living species entry into my garden. And, like Noah, I brought along at least two of them.

Planning? Planning, the most fundamental virtue of all sober gardeners—but that was the problem; I *wasn't* sober!—for me consisted of going to the gardening section of a large grocery store in Nîmes and being frequently and rapturously seduced by the color photographs on the front of seed packets. Then there was a fateful trip to the sprawling nursery in the nearby village of Cadière. I was out of control at the nursery. I wandered among the eye-boggling number of small green choices as if I were at an open, horticultural buffet. I walked into the incubating hothouses with their vast array of little plants and, holding an open cardboard box, chose—everything.

"What are those?" I asked the owner, a big, taciturn farmer who also happened to be the mayor of Cadière.

"Green pepper plants." He waited impatiently.

"Fantastic. I'll take two." Into my cardboard box they went. "And *those*?"

"Hot pepper plants." He looked around distractedly. A young couple arrived, and he gave them a short hello.

"Very interesting. Give me two. No, make that three." Into the box. "And what about *that*?"

The mayor said a word in French I didn't understand.

"Hmmm," I said. "I don't know what that translates to in English. But what the heck. I'll take one. Better make that two, just in case. And what about those plants over there?"

"Zucchini." He was beginning to sound pressed.

"Zucchini? Well, we can't have too much zucchini, can we? Not in the south of France. Give me— four. Wait! Better make that six. Say, this box is getting full. I'd better go get another."

I put the full box down and went to look for an empty one. "You know," I said to Iggy, who had been on her own buying binge at the other end of the nursery and proudly showed me a boxful of strange plants, "all this stuff is amazingly cheap."

We shoved the open boxes of plants into the back of the car. "Do you think we bought too much?" I asked Iggy.

"Well . . . maybe," she said.

We shook hands with the mayor and said goodbye. I was thinking of asking his advice, but he was already talking to another customer even as he released my hand from his huge grip.

All this by way of saying that ultimately I planted the following in the garden at St. Sébastien: Five varieties of lettuce. Three varieties of tomatoes. Zucchini. Eggplant. Basil. Parsley. String beans. Lima beans. Hot peppers. Green peppers. Red peppers.

Yellow peppers. Carrots. Radishes. Melons. Beets. Cabbage. Chives. And two kinds of flowers, one of which was the dwarf sunflower. And not just a few of each plant. An *abundance*. As I look back, I know I should have practiced a kind of gardening birth control. But I didn't. I was delirious.

Shortly after this rampage of inclusion, I went and finished preparing the land, freeing it of any weeds left and raking away clods. The earth, as I said before, was clayey and, when dry, prone to cake and form fist-sized clods as hard as lava. When it had enough water, the land was easy enough to work. When it lacked water, it was a dry demon. I also marked off boundaries to the garden with four stakes. That simple gesture brought an instant order to the land. The dimensions of the garden were roughly thirty feet by forty feet, though in places its frontiers were far from true.

As I write this, it is raining outside. It reminds me of the day in late April—far too early—when I put the first plants into my garden. It was a cool, gray, misty day, one of those damp days when every plant and shrub looks well fed and full of capacity, with water cascading off bent broad leaves so green, so clear and forceful in the dull light. Such watery days uplift a gardener's spirit.

Iggy and I drove our car from the village and, just past the little bridge, turned off the road onto the lane that ran next to the vineyard. In the back of the car was a boxful of plants. The other plants we'd bought at the nursery waited back at the house, resting comfortably in a sun-drenched entranceway indoors, warm and well watered. We were taking eggplant and zucchini, delicate little versions of themselves. I had been told by the villagers that it was too early to plant anything. But I couldn't wait. I had to put something into the earth, into my earth.

I am thinking now of how serious gardeners must be shaking their heads at my lack of restraint, among other misdemeanors. What can I say? Not much, really. That I would do it all differently if I had a chance to do it over again? No. What would be the point of that? Why would I ever deny myself my precious mistakes?

We walked over to the bank. The clayey earth gave way under our feet. The faint mist swayed lightly to and fro, influenced by a slight breeze. In the distance we could see an enclave of stone houses, not enough of them to be considered a village but nevertheless a little world unto itself. A path of smoke rose languidly from one of the chimneys. We walked down the bank and crossed the stream. The water was high from the previous night's rain, and so the boards Jules and I had used to make a bridge felt tentative, ready to float off. We stepped across them gingerly. Then we walked to the far rise, climbed it, and stepped onto the land. The only sound, aside from our mucky footsteps and spoken words, was the dripping of water from leaf to leaf in the small trees and bushes that bordered the land, a soft, slapping sonata.

There was the cleared land before me, a groomed virgin piece of earth, fertile and ready. It was a peaceful moment, and a perfect time to work.

We put the box down on the ground. I had carried some tools with me, too. I had a large shovel, a small hand shovel and a grater. I bent down and felt the earth. It was pliant and moist. I gathered up a handful. It was cool and made a tobacco-colored stain on my hand. Holding freshly-turned dirt is such a pleasure.

"Ready?" I asked Iggy. She stood there in her jeans and sweatshirt. She had on a pair of work gloves, and her dark hair jutted out from a red bandanna.

"Ready," she said.

"Well, what shall we plant first?"

"Zucchini?" she suggested, her dark eyebrows raised in speculation.

"Eggplant?" I said.

"Eggplant," she confirmed with a bright smile.

I reached down into the box and picked up an eggplant. It was skinny and small, with just one or two leaves, not exactly inspiring. I turned the plastic container upside down, tapped the bottom firmly and released the plant from its temporary home. I put the unevenly-shaped bunch of earth and airy roots onto the ground.

"Here?" I asked Iggy, motioning to a spot of land.

"Sure," she said. "Why not?"

I got to my knees and made a small hole by opening the earth with my hand shovel. The mist was gathering in my hair like a spider's web and some of it was flowing off my eyebrows and down my cheeks. I felt the ground sticking to my knees. I placed the plant in the hole. It leaned slightly to its side.

"Here," I said to Iggy, giving her the hand shovel. "You do the honors." She took off her gloves.

She bent down, a lovely Dutch girl who, like most others from her nation, has plants and flowers in her blood. She placed the earth around the plant deftly, like the sure, natural gardener she was. She pulled back, regarded the little plant, and then made several small but critical adjustments to the earth with her fingers. Watching her work, I felt supremely confident about the plant's future. Iggy stood up and wiped her hands on the side of her jeans. The mist was turning into a light rain. Soon it would be a noise.

We both looked at the thin green plant, skinny and frail as a premature baby. It was now part of our earth, the beginning of our garden. I felt a mixture of pride and responsibility.

"It looks great," I said to Iggy. "It looks wonderful."

Planting

We planted the rest of the plants, one by one, and left them there, resting in their new earth, soon to be drenched by the rain.

I had a garden now.

 BAMBOO

I NEEDED SOME BAMBOO and so had come to
Nasim, the Moroccan farmer who worked for the
rich, unmarried hunchback Léontine Cluze.

The two of them were an odd pair. Léontine was
short and plain and walked with the biased gait
characteristic of hunchbacks. It was as if the large
hump that rose from the right part of her back
weighted her to one side and burdened her walk.
She was extremely wealthy and lived in a palazzo-
like house next to ours. She was also, like many of
those with her affliction, sickly, and she made several journeys to the hospital during our year there.

She was not an easy taskmaster. Iggy worked for her briefly in the fields doing some minor pruning, and said she could be difficult. Léontine often followed the workers down the vineyards saying, *"Vite! Vite!"* Faster! Faster! Nasim, who did most of the work for Léontine, never complained about her. He did his job well, and silently.

Nasim Kebdani. What a strange character he was. How friendly, yet how distant. How concerned, yet how aloof. How unfathomable. How *Moroccan*.

This short, swarthy, mustached man, with his quizzical look and throaty laugh, had a wife and three children and worked as hard as any French-man. But he was not havable as a friend. Not by me, anyhow. Because of his origin and religion, he was a sort of outsider in St. Sébastien—more so to some than to others. I felt a kind of alliance with him as a foreigner. Iggy and Nasim's wife, Faridah, became confidants, spending hours together gossiping over tea while the three Kebdani children clambered over them, pleading for attention. But Nasim, though friendly enough toward me, never offered real friendship. And he kept his feelings about his own apartness to himself.

But that did not keep *me* from talking to *him,* teasing him even, or seeking his advice about my garden. He was a good gardener and extremely generous with me, lending me any tool I wanted, though he could be reluctant to give advice. He had a fine little garden, just outside the village, enclosed by a wall. He even had a shed for his tools. This was part of the bargain he made when he agreed to work for Léontine.

On a balmy, gray June day, I was down by his garden asking him where I could find some bamboo to use as stakes and guides for my tomato plants. Nasim, like every man who had a garden in St. Sébastien, was frugal. He used things over and over, year after year, such as the plastic he insulated certain plants with. And his bamboo. He had about twenty pieces, each near the height of a man, which he staked into the ground and used to support his tomato plants when they grew tall and cumbersome with their own bounty. At the end of the summer, when the tomatoes were finished, he simply dislodged the bamboo stakes from the ground, bundled them up into a group and put them back into his shed. There they rested until they were called up for duty the following year.

But I had none. I needed to find fresh bamboo.

I hovered around Nasim as he watered his parsley. As usual, he was dressed heavily, in two or three sweaters, long pants and hat, even though it was June. I was in shorts. Low music emitted from a pants pocket somewhere where he kept a transistor. He offered me a cigarette. He always did, even though he knew by now that I did not smoke. I declined.

"You want some bamboo?" he said, adjusting the

taut, frizzy parsley. When Nasim spoke French, he rolled his *r*s in the characteristic Arab way. After he spoke, he always asked me, even concerning the simplest matters, if I understood him.

"Yes," I said.

"You want some bamboo?"

"Yes, Nasim. Bamboo."

"Good. Do you know Monsieur Albert's house?"

"Yes, I think so."

He turned slowly and pointed outward. "Down past Monsieur Albert's house, toward Gajan-sur-Gardon, there is a small road, off to the left." He looked at me carefully. He wondered if I had understood. "Stop your car there. At the foot of the road. You will see, by the stream. There is all the bamboo you need there."

"And I can cut as much as I want?"

"Yes. As much as you want."

"Thanks. Thanks very much, Nasim."

He placed his open palm softly against his chest, swept his hand upward, and kissed his fingers ever so lightly, a gesture I always found moving.

I got into my Peugeot, waved goodbye to Nasim fanatically, and drove off. As I did, I looked back and saw him, heavily dressed, small and unmoving, standing there in the June day.

I drove out of the village. At the *cave coopérative*, the imposing seventy-five-year-old building where the villagers brought their grapes to be made into wine, I banked left and went down the narrow road that lead to Gajan-sur-Gardon. Nearly three hundred years ago, Catholic soldiers of Louis XIV pursued the Protestant leader Jean Cavalier through Gajan-sur-Gardon, only to be ambushed by Cavalier's band a few kilometers away. My garden was very near a large stone monument that marked the encounter where 322 soldiers were slaughtered by Cavalier—"like flies," as he says in his *Memoirs*. What he doesn't say is that a few days later reinforcements from the crown arrived and forced the villagers of St. Sébastien de Caisson to bury the putrifying bodies. When I walked those fields, I was always hoping to find a bullet, a sword, a skull. I never did.

And when I tramped those fields, I thought much about Jean Cavalier, the astonishing man who began life as a shepherd in this part of France and who died a British army officer with the rank of major general. But I thought more often of the pathos of religion and how particularly cruel those times had been after 1685 when Louis XIV saw fit to revoke the Edict of Nantes. Protestants were forced to convert or die, often horribly, unless they hid or fled. Much of this brutality took place on land I was walking, or nearby in the Cévennes Mountains. It is described with deep feeling by Jean-Pierre Chabrol in his novel *Les fous de Dieu, Those Mad for God*, a mysterious book written as if by a young Protestant living in those times. St. Sébastien today is about half Protestant and half

Catholic, and I often wondered if that provoked any animosity. But each half seemed to coincide tranquilly with the other.

I pulled my car off to the side of the road where Nasim had told me to. A soft breeze was blowing. I walked a few feet toward the stream, and then I saw the bamboo. It was clustered on one side of the stream, and it swayed back and forth slowly in the wind, making a pleasant rustling sound. I was slightly amazed to see bamboo here. It seemed too exotic a plant to be growing among all these plain, monotonous vineyards. But in fact, bamboo was well established in this part of France. A mere twenty-five kilometers away from the vineyards, at the foot of the Cévennes Mountains, was a *bambouserie,* or giant bamboo forest. It was a big tourist attraction.

I walked to the bank. Yes, it was bamboo, all right. It rose about six or seven feet, elegant and slender, lovely beige reeds. I touched them. I felt the wooden length, the sleek, glassy smoothness of the surface. Then I stepped back. I smelled the air. It was sweet and warm. The cloudy, warm day, myself alone by the stream and the rustling of the bamboo leaves made me sad. Tears came to my eyes, and then disappeared almost immediately. I felt a vast loneliness, and I didn't know why. Maybe I was thinking of how quickly my time here in France would end. Maybe it was something I would never know. I took a breath.

I figured I needed about ten pieces. I was carrying a pair of large pruning scissors Nasim had lent me. I bent down, selected one vigorous plant, and cut it. I had expected the bamboo to resist, but it didn't. The scissors gave a slight *whoof* sound as they sliced through, and that was it, the bamboo was cut. The stalk, though, did not fall. Supported by the leaves of its neighbors, it poised. I pushed the stalk forward, and in one easy motion, it fainted, the leaves at the top splaying on the ground as it hit.

Something in me was rattled. I had cut down a thing so beautiful, which had managed to grow so tall.

But I didn't stop. I went on.

I cut my limit. Each time, I heard the sound, *whoof,* as the scissors cut through. *Whoof. Whoof. Whoof.* Ten times, all told. It wasn't an unpleasant sound. I wondered, as I cut, if in ages past the executioner grew to like the easy chop of his beheading ax.

When I had finished, I stripped each plant of its leaves. I felt the regularity of the notches on the stalks. They were like vertebrae, spaced evenly, about every four inches. But what was sustaining this plant? I looked inside where I had made my cut. It was completely hollow. It had no pulp, no veins, just *air*. How could it grow so well?

I carried the ten pieces to my car. They were like enormous chopsticks in my arms. Once or twice they became highly unbalanced, and I staggered and weaved back and forth trying to restore order, like Charlie Chaplin careening about in one of his reckless ballets. Finally, I got them all in the back of my car. I thrust them well forward, over the passenger seat and against the front window. I left the hatchback open and then drove off to the garden with the freshly-cut bamboo dangling far beyond the back of the Peugeot. All that was missing was an OVERSIZED LOAD sign.

I wanted to show Nasim my handiwork. I felt somehow I had become legitimate as a gardener with all this bamboo. I don't know why. I drove slowly, the warm wind brushing across me, my arm dangling out the window, my foot lazily touching only the edge of the accelerator.

After parking the car by the vineyard, I carried the bamboo to the garden and set it down. I had already planted the tomato plants a few weeks earlier, but they were still very small. The bamboo wouldn't really be needed until later when the plants were much taller and had become gangly. Then they would be attached by pieces of soft cloth rags to the bamboo stakes for support. But I couldn't wait until then. I had to put the bamboo in now. It was important. I needed the formality of having the bamboo installed.

107

I watered the ground next to the plants and waited a few minutes for it to soak in and for the earth to become spongy. Then, plant by plant, I inserted each bamboo stake into the earth as deeply as it would go, pushing down with all my might. The bamboo went in at least a foot, maybe more. A few pieces splayed at the tip with my force, but most held perfectly.

It was harder work than I had expected, and when I finished, my chest was heaving, and the sweat poured down my cheeks. But there they stood, like sentinels. They gave a wonderful height to the garden. They *elevated* it, literally and metaphorically. I took a moment to look at the slightly uneven row of tan reeds. My tomato plants looked insignificant next to them all, but I didn't care. Throughout that summer, the bamboo gave unstinting support to those tomato plants. Even when the cruel wind from the Rhône Valley came and blew with all its force, they stood firm.

So far as I know, they're still there, tall, insubstantial, powerful. Waiting.

ROUTINES

EVERYTHING ELSE about my garden was good
and sometimes even thrilling, but this was what *gardening* was: The soft sound of the shovel thrusting
into and dislodging the earth. Feeling the warmth of
the sun on my shoulders. The earth against my knees.
Savoring the undisturbed hours of solitary work. I
didn't need to speak. I didn't need to worry about
opinions or politics. I didn't need anything. I slowly
moved down a row, attending to each plant thoroughly, pushing my shovel in, lifting up the French
soil, getting the backs of my hands dirty, sweating,
wiping the drops from my eyes. Working. I was there
for one simple reason: to help make things grow.

I would usually go to the garden twice a day. Once in the early morning to weed and grate and to do any other work that needed to be done. And once in the evening to water. I left anywhere from six-thirty to seven-thirty A.M., just when the village women were gathering in the square to wait for the first truck, which brought them their bread, and I usually stayed a few hours. I would drive down the little French road, past the villagers on their way to work in the vineyard, my window open. The morning air would strike me, wake me and bring small tears to my eyes. Every time I made this trip in my car from St. Sébastien to my garden, I was eager.

I had the perfect gardening car: the used white Peugeot 104 we had bought shortly after we arrived. It was a cross between a small station wagon and one of those ladybug-like tiny Fiats. It was a wonderful car, light and obedient, and had a big hatchback, so I could shove just about anything in there—from my gardening tools to bamboo to large bags full of compost Nasim had kindly given me. It was a whiz in the fields—since it wasn't heavy at all, it could go just about anywhere, and did. The Peugeot was just as essential and helpful to my garden as my hoe or hand shovel or bucket. It was *trusty*. And with its torn seats and rust-eaten body, I never fretted when it got muddy inside or out. I became very attached to it. It was hard to sell it when we had to leave. I fe.. as though I was deserting a friend.

Sometimes Iggy would come with me, but more often she would not. There was nothing disputatious about this. She and I both agreed this was *my* garden; besides, she had many pursuits of her own. I preferred working alone anyway. I always have. Gardening seems to me a one-person sort of undertaking. When you have two or three people working in a garden it starts to become a *farm*. But when Iggy did come, it was a kind of luxury. It was exciting—and often very distracting—to have her there beside me.

Seeing the garden for the first time in the day was always inspiring. To step up that ledge and see all my plants spaced evenly apart and all in neat, long rows with beaten paths between them, *comme il faut,* as it should be, was a pretty sight. I would take my gardening tools to the edge of the garden and set them down. I would smell the sweetness of the morning air; it was light, cool and vivid. Everything was breathtakingly serene at this time of day and this far from the village. Unless there was somebody working in the vineyard nearby, I had the land all to myself. Even if there was someone working there, once I got started I abandoned myself to my work. There was no sound, except for an occasional solitary bird calling away in a tune as complex as a melody by Prokofiev.

Of course, I had to make a summary inspection of my plants first. I had to walk down each path—it's interesting that the word *routine* comes from the Old

French word *route,* meaning "beaten path"—and see what progress, if any, my plants had made. And to figure out exactly how, and where, I would spend my time in the garden that day. Would it be grating the earth around my string beans with my little hand shovel, a long, tiresome job? Or if she came with me, would I allow Iggy that privilege while I attached the tomato plants to the bamboo stakes at a higher level, one of my favorite jobs? Or maybe it would be to do some weeding around the parsley—not easy, because the weeds mingled so closely, and there was always a danger of mauling the herb.

Once every two weeks or so, when Iggy came with me to the garden, we would work together all morning, or as long as the heat would allow. She was everything I wasn't as a gardener: confident, knowledgeable, circumspect, thorough and patient. We would work silently, each of us intent. From time to time, I would glance over at her to watch her rise up to wipe the sweat from her long, naked neck and the small bubbles that rested on the top of her lip. She would take a deep breath, bend down, go on. My God, I thought.

The earth always needed grating. *"Il faut toujours gratter!"*—You must always grate!—was a piece of advice I heard all the time from all gardeners in St. Sébastien de Caisson. Because the earth was so clayey, I had to continually work it so the water could seep in and reach the roots. If I didn't, the sun would turn the ground into a serving plate. Before the summer became fatally hot, grating the earth was actually a calming pleasure. Normally, the land would still be slightly humid from the previous night's watering. This made penetrating the earth relatively easy.

I would crouch down on one knee, thrust my hand shovel in and turn the earth up and over, revealing its darker, humid underside. Then I would crumble it slowly in my hands to better allow the plant to breathe. In that sense I felt I had a comradeship with the earth: *I* must be able to breathe, too. To do the best job, I had to grate very close to the plant, continually moving it aside, trying not to hack it with my motions. I was surprised and delighted to find how rough I could be with my plants. I mean that my plants, once they'd established themselves in the soil, and when handled confidently, could be moved aside, pulled at and probed without much worry. Their hold on things was much stronger than I thought. At those moments I remembered Ford, my grandmother's gardener, and thought of his confidence with plants.

The simplest task could produce small moments of despair. Like transplanting. I remember once lifting three crowded but thriving cucumber plants, one already flowering, from the earth, separating their roots from the soil. I teased them out, careful to leave as many spidery roots intact as I could. The plants felt vigorous in my hand, and I remember thinking they were strong enough for the move. I dug three new holes. I inserted each of them, re-covered them with earth, then watered each one. That evening when I returned to water the garden, the three were limp, their leaves pathetically plastered against the earth. I felt as though I'd committed murder.

Working away in the dirt, handling things I'd planted myself, getting into a routine, I enjoyed letting my mind wander. I'd daydream about everything. It was at those times easy to create fantasies or dramas, some very elaborate. I saw in my mind's eye:

Several men appeared at the edge of the garden. Monsieur Céret, Monsieur Noyer and Marcel Lécot. St. Sébastien's best gardeners.

"Richard," said Monsieur Céret, "we've come to see you. Are you busy?"

"No, I'm just working. I'm always glad to see you. What can I do for you all?"

"Richard," Monsieur Noyer said, stepping forward, "I've been a gardener in St. Sébastien for many, many years." He said this with a calm strength.

"Yes, it's true!" Marcel said, laughing and putting his hand on Monsieur Noyer's shoulder. "He's the oldest of us!"

"Every year, I've had a garden," Monsieur Noyer said, "without fail."

"I know," I said. "I've heard. They all speak about you."

He smiled briefly. "But what I want to tell you, Richard"— he passed a hand before him, indicating my land—"is that yours is a garden I myself would be proud of."

Marcel smiled at this. Monsieur Céret nodded. I turned and looked at my garden. "Really?" I heard myself say. "*Really?*"

When I turned back, I looked for them, St. Sébastien's three best gardeners, but they had disappeared. I bent down and went back to work.

At the end of the morning, when the sun's force had made it too hot to work anymore, it was time to go. It was hard to leave the garden sometimes— especially later in the summer when things really began to grow. Then sometimes I stayed on foolishly in the heat, working away, once or twice nearly fainting in the furious noon sun. But it was also satisfying to stand back at the edge of the garden and look at the good work I had done, to see how clear the land looked around the plants that had been weeded and how gratifying the freshly turned earth looked around a row of plants. They had been *tended*.

I would take my pail and shovel and whatever other equipment I had and go back to the car. It was fine, driving back to St. Sébastien after a morning's work in the garden, my arm muscles throbbing a bit, my face beating from the sun, the window open. I was dirty. I was tired. I was sweaty. I was happy.

 SNAILS

ONCE I ARRIVED at the garden early, about six
A.M., after a rain the night before, to find an old
woman there. I had never come upon a stranger in
my garden before.

"Good morning," I said to her. I couldn't imagine that she was stealing any vegetables—only the
lettuce was ripe—but . . .

"Good day," she said absently. She was dressed
shabbily, and her face was worn, marked by the obvious struggle to sustain herself. "I am looking for
snails," she muttered. "I hope this doesn't bother
you." I looked down and saw the torn old burlap

bag in which she was carrying the snails she had gathered. Of course, the rain! Snails always appeared in numbers after it rained, clinging to the underside of the plants' leaves. She had quite a number, I could see, some already frothing their clear bubbles of captivity. Later, I asked the villagers what she would do with them. She would sell them at the market in Uzes for about forty francs the hundred, they said. Not much.

"No, no," I said to her. "You're not bothering anybody. Please come anytime you want." She didn't answer. She continued her search, quickly examining the leaves of my lettuce and muttering. I wondered if she had any family, where she came from, who she was. I bent down to unload my hoe and rake, and when I looked up, she was gone.

All morning long her presence haunted me. I did not feel easy working with the specter of her poverty before me.

But in the end it was my garden she had come to, and so maybe my lettuce, dripping still with the previous night's rain, had provided her with some snails she wouldn't have otherwise found. I hoped so, at least. And after that, I tried not to forget that even the dullest task I had to perform was a luxury.

 WATERING

YOU MIGHT NOT expect something as ordinary as watering would be controversial, but it was. In the south of France, it was. And especially in St. Sébastien de Caisson. The controversy revolved around what time of day to water, morning or evening. This was no very small matter, as it turned out. Actually, I didn't fully understand how important it was until later, when it grew hotter. The villagers were roughly divided in half on this question, and the passion with which each expressed his or her point of view only served to bewilder me. Villagers without gardens also felt free—obliged, I would say—to express themselves openly on the subject.

This was an issue for one simple reason: *le Lion,* the Sun. As the days grew hotter, and even hotter, and the sun turned into a dangerous fire to be respected and feared, it became essential not to water in its presence. How can I convey the sun's relentless brutality now, its "blank and pitiless stare," so many months and so many miles away? The sun, whose lovely light had often caressed us in the winter months, became, during the long summer days, a tireless killer. If, for example, you made the stupid mistake of watering the garden *anytime* after seven A.M., random droplets that splashed onto the leaves would be converted into tiny magnifying glasses, and the sun would sizzle the leaves into a wilted mess.

So from the beginning it had been made clear to me by numerous St. Sébastieners that the question of *when* to water was a profound one. What should I do? Naturally, I first asked Monsieur Noyer. This short, broad-headed man with massive hands, skeptical eyebrows and gray hair was the former president of the *cave coopérative* and St. Sébastien's most celebrated gardener. When I asked him what time to water, he spoke without hesitating.

"You must water at dawn, Richard. Before the sun rises. Then the earth is cool. The roots can better accept the water." He looked at me sharply. This was more than advice. This was a pronouncement.

We were, in fact, in his garden. It was strictly kept, well watered, and produced plants of such health you might see them displayed at the Iowa State Fair.

"Exactly what time should I water, Monsieur Noyer?" I asked.

"Before six-thirty. No later. Even at that hour, you are taking a chance. The sun is already past the horizon." He glanced over to the low hills in the east where the sun came up.

"Wouldn't it be better to water in the evening? After it's cooled down a bit?"

"No! Never!" The words shot out of his mouth like bullets. Since his garden adjoined the town square, they resounded off the town hall, furthering their effect. "Even after the sun has set, the land is still warm." He moved his fingers together cautiously, as if he were feeling the baked earth. "When you water then, it's bad for the roots. It shocks them."

He stepped closer to me and put aside his hoe. "Who told you to water your garden in the evening, Richard?"

"Oh, well . . ." I had to think quickly. "Some-body . . . from another village," I blurted. People from other villages always knew nothing.

He snorted and looked at me carefully. Then he pointed an instructing finger. "Never water in the evening, Richard. Never!"

Watering

Of course, it wasn't somebody from another village who had told me to water in the evening. It
was Marcel Lécot, St. Sébastien's second-best gardener. As I said, Monsieur Noyer was acknowledged
to be St. Sébastien's best gardener, and so his advice
had a weighty authority. But Marcel had his cham-
pions, too; I had seen his garden, and it was impres-
sive. Marcel was a retired plumber who had worked
ten years in Lyon. He disliked Lyon: "It's too big,
Richard! St. Sébastien, it's much better." Marcel was
a balding, robust man, animated and kind, with
burly forearms and a wide, generous smile that con-
founded his seventy-three years. I liked him very
much. He was always friendly to me, and to Iggy.
When we talked, he looked at me intently, his head
tilted slightly to one side, and he had the habit of
mouthing my words with me as I spoke them. It was
as if he wanted to help me somehow in my feeble
efforts at speaking French with some of his boundless
energy, and this always endeared him to me, though
unfortunately it never seemed to help my French.

Marcel felt very strongly that a garden should be
watered in the evening.

"*Exactly* what time in the evening should I water,
Marcel?" We were having our conversation in the
square, next to his house. It was a warm spring day,
and the sun bathed us luxuriously. A car sped down
the road in the distance, its tires spitting out bits of
gravel. We glanced at it. I had already begun to ac-

quire the village habit of noting carefully the most ordinary occurrences.

"Eight o'clock in the evening, Richard," Marcel said. "No earlier. Even later, perhaps."

"That's pretty late."

"The later the better, Richard. The land will guard the water then. Even through the night."

"Why can't I water in the morning, before the sun gets too hot?"

"Never!" He made a step backwards in alarm.

"Why not?" I was startled by his passion.

"At six-thirty the sun rises and—poof!—the heat sucks up all the water." Here he made a pulling-up motion with both hands. "There's nothing left. And if any water gets on the plants' leaves, it can be very bad for them. Very bad." He shook his head seriously. "No, never. Never water in the morning." He peered at me closely to see if I comprehended.

"I see, Marcel," I said. He mouthed those few words with me. Then he nodded. But he was still not convinced.

"Who told you to water in the morning, Richard?"

"Uh . . . nobody, Marcel. Really. I just . . . heard it." It was the truth. I hadn't yet had my audience with Monsieur Noyer. I did, however, already know through my general investigations that some people watered their gardens in the early morning.

Marcel looked at me. It was a dubious look. Then

he slapped me on the shoulder. "Take care, Richard."
He grinned and pointed upward. "The sun!"

What was I going to do? What a dilemma! After
much seeking of advice and much anxiety over the
question—even the man who sold me my newspaper
in a nearby town had an opinion; everyone did!—
I decided to water in the evening, when the power
of the scorching sun had abated. It suited my tem-
perment better, for one thing. And I found the land
did guard the water—even though it was still warm
when I arrived—all through the night and far into
the next morning. And I could splash the leaves in-
advertently, without fear. Thus began my ritual. At
eight o'clock every evening, when the sun was just
beginning to set, I went and watered my garden.

Monsieur Noyer didn't let this most crucial decision pass unnoticed, however. Whenever he saw me
loading my car in the evening, obviously on my way
to the garden, he would look at me for a few dev-
astating seconds, snort, and glance away. He always
made me feel as if I had disobeyed the Master. And I
always wondered if I made the wrong decision about
watering, especially when my plants began to suffer
from the violent heat.

Watering my garden was not easy. It was a complicated, laborious job and a frustrating one. Since
my land was away from the town, I had no *robinet,*
no faucet that provided ready water. I did have a

stream that flowed near my land, but it ran in a ravine about ten feet below the plot, off to one side. So there was only one way to get the water: by hand. The main device in this process was a thick, fifteen-liter green rubber bucket Jules had loaned me. I simply attached a rope to its handle, tossed it the ten feet or so below into the stream and then pulled it back up, full. This required a certain technique. If the bucket was tossed out just any way, the bottom would probably strike the water first and the bucket would remain floating—i.e., remain empty. I had to learn to toss the bucket outward in such a way that, falling downward, its rim would strike the water first and cut into the stream, allowing water to enter and sink the bucket. After hauling it back up, I carried the full bucket—or nearly full, since some water always sloshed out on the way up—to the garden and watered my plants.

Now the obvious question is: Why didn't I rig up some sort of pulley system? Or go and buy a pump, even a primitive one? I had no money for a pump. And even if I had, spending so much money for a pump to grow my own vegetables *just one time* seemed a bit indulgent. Especially when you could buy beautiful things in the market so cheaply. The central idea here wasn't to save money, I agree; but it wasn't to waste it, either. As for pulleys, well, even if I could have *found* a hook and tackle, it wouldn't have worked. As I said, no bucket simply lowered would have picked up water. The stream was not moving fast enough to tilt the bucket by itself.

Generally, the entire process, including the hauling and the actual watering, took about an hour. By the end of that hour, the bank was slippery from spilt water, and I was exhausted. My back and arms were aching, not only from hauling dead weight, but from the forced angles I had to place my body in to keep the bucket from banging against the side and spilling as it was pulled up. The process then became very tricky. I nearly slid off the muddy bank and into the stream several times. Once I actually did slide off, rescuing myself like Harold Lloyd grabbing the arm of that huge clock. I grasped an exposed tree root that grew nearby. I wish I had a photograph of that moment.

Even though it was difficult and time-consuming, I loved to water my plants. There was something eminently satisfying about giving *water* to them. I hesitate to use the word spiritual, but. . . . I loved the pure, colorless liquid, spraying out from my vessel and splashing to the ground, this strange substance that made things grow. It was mysterious to me. And still is.

There were times when, for whatever reason—a dinner at someone's house or a visit to another village—that I couldn't water my garden until very late. Sometimes I arrived at my garden as late as midnight—once, even at two-thirty A.M. If there was no moon, then I turned my car toward the garden and left my headlights on. The two Peugeot beams more or less provided enough illumination to work by, though one was astigmatic, and so it sprayed its light a bit wildly into the tops of bushes.

If there was a full moon, though, I didn't need to use my car lights.

Watering my garden late on a soft summer night in the empty French countryside was a rapturous experience. As the moon led me, I walked back and forth to the bank near the stream, threw my bucket in, and hauled up bucket after bucket of cool water from the stream. I couldn't see the stream, or the bucket when it landed, but I could hear the splash. Once they got used to me, the frogs continued their mad barking and gave me my metronome. The air was remarkably soft.

The light from the moon was just strong enough so most of the time I didn't trip over a root or a bulging stone. But the glow was also just weak enough to blur outlines of trees and bushes and make it difficult to judge distances properly. Was that plant ten feet away from me, or two? Was that a basil plant or an eggplant? Moonlight is a light that's not quite there, like the red light in the darkroom of a photographer. It was all like a dream. I often felt my life in St. Sébastien was like a dream, and this moonlit ritual only made it seem more so. But there was something wonderfully subterranean about it all. Being at my garden so late, guided only by the light of the moon, was like working in a pale, white sea, and my motions, somewhat tentative and groping, made me feel as if I were swimming in the night.

 # STAIRS

IT WAS BACK in April. Everything was still wet and cool, soaked with promise. In order to get to my land, I had to descend a bank, cross a little stream and ascend another bank. These banks were grassy. In the morning, when they were covered with dew— or after a rain—they were slippery and perilous, particularly if I had an armful of gardening tools. Despite my caution, I had already fallen more than once. One time a shovel had nearly impaled me.

"We will have to build stairs," Jules said as we stood at the bottom of the bank on a fresh, damp morning. He was there, of course, because once again, I had asked him for his help.

"Stairs?" I said.

"*Bien sûr,*" he said.

"But . . . how?" I looked wildly around.

He regarded me with that combination of surprise and pity I saw in his face when he discovered yet again how unknowing an American could be. Then he motioned for me to follow him to his car. I could only picture something out of an Ethan Allen furniture store.

"My grandfather built stairs at the edge of his garden," he said, opening his car door. "We will build yours the same way." Jules adored his grandfather, that rugged farmer in his seventies who still went every day to the fields. When he spoke about him, his eyes might water slightly. "*C'est un dur,*" he'd say as the old man passed by on his *mobilette*. He's a tough one. Often when I had a question about the garden, Jules would simply tell me, "Go see how my grandfather has done it."

We drove back to Jules's house and got shovels, an ax, small lengths of wood. Back at the bank again, he made many calculations, measuring the earth and wood carefully. Then we—well, he—hacked his ax into the side of the moist ground. These stairs, I realized at last, were to be made only from the earth. I stood there in the wet, cool April day, observing

129

Jules work. As always, it was an inspiring sight. He was overwhelmingly strong, and he made the most arduous tasks look easy. After we had become friends, we had our mandatory male muscle comparisons, our posings. And our arm wrestlings. That was when I discovered the awesome force of his long forearms, the muscles encouraged by those hundreds of hours snapping dense grapevine branches with his pruning scissors in that classic sideways motion. He *crushed* me. A faint smile crossed his lips, I remember, as my feeble American forearm slammed to the table.

Jules cut out large oval portions of the grassy earth—they looked like dark heads with wet, green hair—and hacked three ascending indentations into the bank. Next, he beat and hewed the newly-cut ground into exact plateaus. Finally, he hammered in the short pieces of lumber upright into the sides as support. After a while, when it appeared to me that the stairs were done, I said:

"The stairs are *formidable*."

As he hammered a stake even further into the earth next to the stairs, he said without pausing, "They're not finished yet."

"No?"

"Of course not."

Of course not! Each earthen plateau had to be honed with an ax, so it was nearly as shiny and smooth as wooden stairs. These stairs of mine, two

kilometers from the village, in the middle of a vineyard, unseen by the world, would be used by only a
few people—and mostly just by me—but they had
to be done right. Finally, Jules stood back, looked at
his work carefully, and gave a brief nod of approval.
"Done," he said. They were beautiful stairs. Any
mason would have been proud to admit they were
his. They were so superbly fashioned, I am certain
they exist still today.

And each time my foot hit them, I felt secure,
and reassured, carrying my tools. I *bounded* up those
stairs, feeling beneath my feet the solid flatness chis-
eled out of the earth. I came to the garden throughout the spring and summer with an extra burst of
energy because of the literal support Jules had given
me. I was inspired by the pride this man had put into
his work. I thought of how demanding he was, in a
good way, about things. And how the stairs were the
result of his uncompromising way of working.

When I was around Jules, I strove to meet certain standards. I believed I had a responsibility to
try and make my garden something he would himself be proud of. I wanted to show this man who
had allowed an outsider into his world that I *could*
garden in France, in St. Sébastien de Caisson. That
I *could* sweat and dig and care as well as another. I
feared disappointing Jules. Sounds odd, sounds so
wrong an emotion—fear—for so pastoral a pursuit
as a garden. But the fear was real, I can assure you.

131

My fear of disappointing Jules was at times as much a motivation in my garden as the simple pleasure of making things grow. I wanted this twenty-year-old to be proud of me.

TOOLS

EVERYTHING I USED in the garden, all my tools and implements, I borrowed. Everything except for my small hand shovel, which Iggy bought for me and which I have today, here in New York. It still has some French dirt caked on it. I've made no effort to clean it.

Though I was shy about borrowing at first, I soon realized that the villagers weren't reluctant to lend me things. Anyway, I didn't have the money to buy any of the magnificent tools, black with newness, I would see at the *quincaillerie,* or hardware store, in Nîmes. I borrowed tools from Nasim, Jules, Monsieur Noyer and Monsieur Valcoze. And I felt closer to them because of it. And always will. What did they lend me? Shovel, rake, hoe, grater, bucket. Classic instruments of labor. They were tools that had been used for years, whose handle lengths, full of small hills and valleys, were varnished and slippery from years of sweaty manhandling. Real tools.

Using these tools every day was very satisfying to me. I loved taking them from their resting place in the *cave,* loading them in the car, hearing the sounds they made jostling together as I drove along. I loved carrying the tools from the car to the garden under my arm. When the Peugeot broke down at one point, and I had to go to the garden on our *mobilette,* I would strap the hoe and rake to the side of the bike, their lengths exceeding the bike's by at least a foot. Sometimes, the straps would gradually loosen, and I would be forced to drive the motorbike with one hand while trying, with the other, to keep the slowly dipping tools from striking the moving ground and upending me. Fortunately, there was never much traffic.

My favorite tool, which I had borrowed from Nasim, was a hoe. When I hacked into the ground to make a new furrow, I thought of how the hoe was probably one of the least-changed tools in history. That slim blade, bent the angle of a beaver's tooth, at the end of a good staff of whorled wood, is all a hoe is. Simple. But so useful! Hardly anything was better for chopping up patches of weeds in my garden. Or for tearing apart a new piece of earth. I saw Nasim perform the most finite adjustments to the earth surrounding his plants with his hoe, using deft, rapid, abridged movements. I always watched him carefully when he had his hoe in his hands. The hoe was a tool that took to the broadest, most physical gestures, swings and strikes. It was one that could also, in the hands of a Nasim Kebdani, inch next to a parsley plant, disturbing the ground in delicious little chops, without making the plant so much as quiver. Every time I use a hoe, I think of Nasim.

Next to the hoe, I valued my hand shovel the most. There is a story to that, one that revealed a bit about Iggy, and which surprised me.

In a garden, a hand shovel is indispensible. A great deal of the garden's daily upkeep, the work, can be accomplished with this tool—the cutting into, breaking up and sifting of the earth and scores of nameless essential tasks. It was not a common tool, though, among the gardeners in St. Sébastien—they preferred to use a hoe for most everything—and so I had to buy my own. I bought a succession of cheap, tinny hand shovels, costing about a dollar apiece. Sooner or later, each bent over onto itself, revealing just how cheap it was. As this happened again and again, I grew more frustrated. I couldn't work!

I would often come home from the garden early, discouraged, and after a while, even before I said a word, Iggy, seeing my face, came to know why.

It was obvious I needed something better. I had seen a beautiful hand shovel in the gardening section of the supermarket in Nîmes, but it was too expensive, twenty dollars, perhaps. One day, however, Iggy went shopping, and when she returned, she brought the shovel out of the bag and handed it to me.

"Wow," I said, turning it over in my hand, feeling its heaviness and solidness. Then I looked at her.

"Iggy?"

"Yes."

"We can't afford this."

She smiled a sly, introverted smile. "Sure. It was too expensive."

"So how . . . ?"

"Don't worry about it. You needed it, didn't you? I got it for you. Don't worry about 'so how.'" She smiled the same little smile.

"But, Iggy . . ." I knew that smile. It wasn't one of selfless sacrifice. Had she . . . ?

"You like it?" she said, taking the shovel from me. "It's a good one, isn't it?"

"Yes, but . . . ," I began, without conviction.

"So use it."

This woman was the reason that I was in France. She was one of the most courageous people I'd ever met—she was afraid of confronting no one—yet she also had a somewhat eccentric way of reasoning at times, and that was coupled with a will of titanium. Once she had made up her mind, you might as well submit. But I couldn't think of anyone I'd rather have with me to turn around an unknown corner, in an unknown land.

I took the shovel. And I used it. With ardor.

In fact, aside from this one luxury, I didn't need much to garden in France. Just a shovel, a rake, a hoe, a pail. Some bits of cloth to secure my tomato plants. Bamboo. A few wooden stakes for boundaries. A cup of coffee in the morning, maybe, to get me going. That and the land, of course. My clothes were just as simple. I wore jeans and a sweatshirt at the start, in April, shorts and a T-shirt later when it got hot. And a cap. I used gloves once in a while, mainly with the hoe. The sleek wooden handle could raise a blister quickly. I didn't want to be prevented from working because of that. Otherwise, I wanted to feel the earth, so I dispensed with the gloves. I had borrowed them, too.

When I think of my shovel, or my bucket, or any of the tools I borrowed, I think of the many pleasures I had doing simple labor. And I see a picture of myself. I'm in my garden, working with my hoe. It is morning. Early summer. The sun is steadily rising. I move slowly forward. I lift the hoe, raise it above me. It pauses above my head in that brief, gravityless instant between cause and effect. When I strike, the earth erupts slightly under my force. I feel as if I'm entering the land. I look up. I've got a bit of a way to go. And all morning ahead of me.

 # TOMATOES

I SAW MONSIEUR NOYER out of the corner of my eye, approaching me. It was a warm day in mid-June. The sun splashed down on the empty square. I was in the midst of loading my car with my hoe, rake, shovel and other tools, getting ready to go to the garden.

"Eh, Richard," Monsieur Noyer said when he reached me. "And the garden? How goes it?"

"It's going very well, Monsieur Noyer," I said. "Very well. I'm working hard."

"And your tomatoes?" he went on. "Do you have any tomatoes yet?"

"No, not yet." I smiled at his little dig. It was much too early to have tomatoes. "No tomatoes *yet*. But the plants look good. And they're growing."

He raised his hand, a thick farmer's paw, and tipped back his hat. This sixty-plus-year-old French farmer was a far better gardener than I probably would ever be, but there was a kind of rivalry going on here. Perhaps that is much too presumptuous. But there *was* something territorial at least. He was, remember, acknowledged to be St. Sébastien's best gardener.

"Have you treated your tomato plants?" he asked.

At the far edge of the big square, and bathed in cool morning shadows, was Monsieur Noyer's pleasant house. Out on the terrace I could see his wife, Madame Noyer, a short, slightly bent woman, busy with something. Every so often she stopped and regarded us, leaning forward and straining, unsuccessfully, to hear what we were saying. Then she would resume her work.

"Uh, no," I answered. "Do I have to?"

He let out a low whistle. Then he cleared his throat. "You haven't treated your tomato plants with sulphur?" he asked.

"Sulphur?"

"Sulphur. Yes."

"What's that for? Insects?"

"No. No. The treatment is for disease."

"Oh."

He examined me. Then he sniffled and rubbed his mouth with the back of his enormous hand. He looked up at the sky.

"Well . . . to work," he said as a way of saying goodbye. He turned and walked away. After a few steps he paused and looked back.

"You will see, Richard," he said, pointing a low finger. "Gardening is an art. An *art*."

He walked off. His wife stopped her work and watched him approach the house. I was left standing there, in the empty square, full of doubts. Doubts about my tomato plants.

This wasn't the first time we had talked about my tomatoes. Each time we did, it made me nervous. There was usually something slightly cautionary in Monsieur Noyer's tone. He was never malicious, but he acted as if he knew something I didn't. Of course, since I knew almost nothing, it didn't take much effort to make me feel that way. I think he was just probably suspicious that I, as an American, could be serious about gardening—which to him was indeed a serious matter. I respected that. But whatever the reason, these impromptu meetings we had from time to time always left me anxious. I tried to avoid Monsieur Noyer without seeming rude.

The irony was that when it came to the produce from his own garden, he and his wife were extremely generous. They were always handing us sprawling heads of lettuce and other vegetables, or leaving these delights just outside our door. They even gave us some artichokes once, a lovely treat, since they didn't have many. Still, I have to confess that I wanted to outshine Monsieur Noyer in some small effort—peppers, maybe. I felt competitive, and that was not good, not when it was about a garden. I learned a small, unpleasant truth about myself through Monsieur Noyer.

Tomatoes. I was thinking about tomatoes.

For some reason, everyone in the village saw tomatoes as the benchmark for determining the success of my garden, or any garden. Anyone in St. Sébastien who asked about my garden, and many of them did, inevitably asked me about my tomatoes.

Hey, Richard! How many tomato plants did you plant? Twenty? All hybrids? Ah, well. I don't know. You may get a few.

Richard. How far apart did you plant your tomatoes? Oh? Really? Hmmmm.

Richard, just remember. If your tomatoes don't grow, you can have some of ours. We'll have plenty.

Why tomatoes? I suppose because tomatoes are the one thing any serious gardener is expected to grow and one which, ultimately, is not that difficult to grow. And it's emblematic of the south of France. You *must* have tomatoes if you have a summer garden here—fat, nearly obese, crimson things that have a wonderful weight in the hand. Dark, ripe tomatoes that, reeking with the sun, heat and land, are the essence of summer and one of its chief joys. Of course, tomatoes!

Believe me, I watched my tomato plants well. I plucked tiny, errant sprouts from the crotches of the stalks. I attached the vines to my bamboo at regular intervals, careful not to cut off the circulation with too tight a knot in the rag when I did. I dug up the earth around the plants to make it easier for them to breathe and accept water. I even treated them with sulphur as Monsieur Noyer said I should, something I wasn't enthusiastic about doing. (It was, in fact, the only chemical I ever used in my garden. But since *every* gardener in St. Sébastien used it, I did, too.) There was hardly a time when I wasn't thinking about my tomato plants, or tending them.

Once in a while, I would take a villager to my garden to get his opinion on how I was doing. If he didn't say anything much, why, I assumed I wasn't doing anything radically wrong. No one ever looked at my tomato plants and screamed, Oh, my *God!* What have you done? (Not that that would be their style.) I wanted to show off, too. Over here, I wanted to tell them. Just take a look at these tomato plants. Twenty of them. They're healthy-looking, and they're growing nicely. Not too bad for an American in France. And I believe I will have tomatoes, in August, like you.

In late June, a week or so after my conversation with Monsieur Noyer, I drove my car one morning

143

to the garden to do some weeding and grating. By then I had made the trip scores and scores of times, but I still always enjoyed it. The morning air was sweet and cool. I had my bucket and tools with me, the windows open. I passed by farmers on their way to and from the vineyards. Some ambled slowly by on their tractors, others went by in battered old cars they used for the fields. I waved to them, and they waved back. I honked the horn as I passed by Jules's house. His mother was hanging out the wash. She turned and looked toward the sound slightly mystified, then waved as she recognized my car. I picked up speed as I left the village.

I reached the familiar little bridge and turned off the road onto the lane next to the vineyard. I stopped at my usual place, took out my tools, and walked over the edge of the bank. I walked down the steps Jules had fashioned out of the earth and then over the heavy planks I had placed across the stream and which I had christened *Pont de Jules*, Jules's Bridge. As I did, the sleek frogs that had been sunbathing on the planks fled into the water. I walked over to the rise at the edge of the plateau. I was eager to see what progress my plants had made. I was expectant, as always.

I climbed the second set of steps, reached the garden and blinked my eyes. I blinked again. Then my heart skipped a beat. Each one of my twenty tomato plants had a ripe red tomato there at its base!

Tomatoes

I couldn't believe it. I had tomatoes! You could see them. It was a miracle!

I shouted "Tomatoes!" in the air. The word resounded into the heavens. Then I put my bucket down and ran over to the far side of the garden where all the tomato plants were. I had tomatoes. *In June!* As I came closer, though, something inside me started doubting. Isn't it a bit odd, a small voice inside me said, that every one of the twenty plants has produced a single ripe tomato? And only *one*? And that each tomato is at exactly the same place?

Suddenly, I realized someone had put them all there.

I laughed. I laughed so hard I nearly fell down. What a trick! I got to the plants, and, yes, it was true. Someone had obviously gone to the store, bought twenty ripe tomatoes—from Spain, no doubt—and placed them neatly one by one at the base of each of my plants. *American needs help. Bad. With his tomatoes.* I looked around quickly to see if the culprit was there, hiding behind a bush, stifling a laugh. No, I was alone. As I looked around, though, I saw there was more to this. That same person had placed tin cans of string beans on each side of my bean plants. I looked at those cans with their labels displaying cut, juicy string beans, and I laughed again. This was amazingly, heroically funny. This was genius.

I had to show Iggy this masterpiece, this astonishing visual drollness. I didn't touch a thing. I wanted her to see everything exactly as I did. The joke was on me, and I loved it.

Who had done this?

I went back to St. Sébastien, thinking about that question the entire way. It mystified me. The joke was so witty, so dry, and that was not typical of the villagers. Or maybe it was. Maybe I had underestimated them, didn't really know them that well at all. I went and found Iggy and told her we had to go to the garden, now. I wouldn't tell her why. When we got there, I made her cover her eyes as I led her up the stairs. Then I showed her. She was just as fooled as I was for a minute. I could tell by her eyes. Then she walked closer and saw the set-up. *"Nou, zeg!"* she said in Dutch. Now, say! She automatically reverted to Dutch when something took her by surprise. Then she laughed. It was still as funny as when I saw it the first time. Tomato, tomato, tomato. *Twenty* ripe tomatoes, all in a row.

We speculated as to who had done it. We could only think of one name.

"Eugène," we both said at once. Eugène was Jules's younger brother. He was a habitual and determined trickster.

We drove back to the village and, after a short search, we found Eugène.

"Eugène, did you do this?" I asked.

"Do what?"

"You know," Iggy said to him.

"I don't know what."

"Come on," we said.

"You're both crazy."

Eugène denied our accusations so convincingly, we decided it couldn't be him. We told the story to all the villagers we saw and asked them if they knew who had done it. No one knew. But they were amused. Very amused.

We ran into Monsieur Vasquez, who was patrolling the town square as usual, chewing on his small wooden stick and limping slowly along.

"Monsieur Vasquez," I asked, "have you heard anything about the ripe tomatoes in our garden?"

"Tomatoes? Ripe? No."

"Not one word?" Iggy probed.

"No."

"Well, if you do, let us know, will you?" I said.

"Yes." He looked at us oddly.

We ran into Nasim. He knew nothing, but laughed loudly, showing his blackened teeth unreservedly when we explained the situation in our garden. I even asked Albin Polge, the mayor, if he had any ideas about this, but he shook his head, seriously, no. He offered to make an inquiry over the loud-speaker—which was perched atop the town hall—at noon, the customary time for announcements, but I declined. He rubbed his chin with his hand speculatively and said, more to himself, "Ripe tomatoes." Then he produced a slight smile. The mayor had a dry sense of humor.

Did Rèmy, who lived next to Marcel Lécot, know? No. Did Monsieur Valcoze? No. But he did want to talk to me about another matter. . . . Did Sully Valcoze know? Why, no, Richard, no. By the way, he asked in his woody voice, how *was* the garden?

All the people we talked to, and we talked to quite a few in the next two hours, knew nothing. What a mystery!

A little later, still in the dark as to who had done this, I saw Monsieur Noyer. I was in front of the house with Iggy, unloading the car, when I saw him approach. I paused and waited for him to arrive.

"Eh, Richard," he said, tipping his hat back. "And your garden? How goes it?"

"Beautiful, Monsieur Noyer," I said, almost routinely. Then something struck me like a thunderbolt. I waited a beat. "I've got tomatoes," I said to him. "Ripe tomatoes. Now."

He blinked. Then he had such a childlike look of open disappointment, I was almost sorry I'd said it.

"Tomatoes, you say?" he said. "Ripe?"

148

"Absolutely," I said. "And not just one, *twenty* of them."

"Oh?" he said. "Twenty? Really? Very good."

He couldn't conceal on his face what this information meant to him. Iggy saw this. She nudged me in the ribs.

"You've got to tell him the truth," she whispered forcefully in English. *"Now.* Just look at his face!"

Do I have to? I thought. Oh, what a low character I am!

But of course I told him. I told him it was all a joke someone had played on me. That in fact I didn't have any tomatoes, not even one. When he heard this, he shifted easily and quickly back to his familiar, commanding presence. Everything was all right again. The world was exactly as it should be.

We finally found out who had done it. Laurent Imbert! The most unlikely person in the whole village. A calm, introverted man who, though very pleasant to us, never displayed much of a sense of humor— much less such an elaborate one. But it was he. True, Iggy had worked for him harvesting asparagus, but we hadn't thought to call him till last. I hardly knew him. But we cornered him on the telephone. When he was still at the stage of good-naturedly denying he had placed the tomatoes there, I said to him:

"Well, if you didn't put them there, how *did* they get there?"

He waited a long beat, his timing perfect. "Perhaps," he said deadpan, "they are a new variety."

When I stopped laughing, I had the presence of mind to ask him if he needed any "ripe" tomatoes.

No, he said, quite evenly, no, he didn't. I could hear his wife laughing in the background.

I never thought the same way about the villagers again. I certainly learned that some of them could be very funny. Oddly, I never thought to ask Laurent *why* he had done this. It didn't occur to me! I just thought it was funny. I'm sure he thought it was, too. That he didn't know me too well, and still chose my garden to act out his joke, I found endearing. My "ripe" tomatoes went on to become legendary in the village. I was always asked—by men, women and even children in St. Sébastien—if my tomatoes were ripe yet, usually followed immediately by a hand placed to the mouth to stifle laughter. I didn't mind. Why should I? Wasn't teasing a form of affection?

But, oh, Monsieur Noyer, I ask your forgiveness now! Pardon me for taking advantage of you, for seizing what surely was a once-in-a-lifetime moment. Just for the briefest time I had you believing *l'américain* had outdone you. That somehow, I, the American, had pulled off a tomato miracle in St. Sébastien de Caisson!

 SEEDS

I HAD PLANTED melons for Madame Basselier in her fields, and she had given me some extra seeds when I told her I had a garden. Madame Basselier was a French woman right out of a Rubens painting, rosy-cheeked, ample-breasted, nearly plump, with a good smile, and I was a little in love with her. How she would be shocked by that! While her husband used the more intimate *tu* form for *you* with me almost immediately, she never did. When I asked her about this once, she said, "It takes me a long time before I can do that, Richard. There are people in

St. Sébastien I have known for *twenty-five years*"—the
emphasis was hers—"and I still say *vous* to them"—
referring to the more formal way of saying *you* in
French.

Madame Basselier and her husband, Roland, lived
in a little *mas,* or farm, about a half kilometer from
the village. It was a world of its own, and I used to
love to go there, even if it meant I would be working very hard in their fields or vineyards. They had
cherry trees and apricot trees and fig trees and a tree
that produced a fruit which I had never seen before that had the taste and texture of a leechee nut
and which was delicious. They were always generous
about letting me pick and eat my fill.

My working for the Basseliers resulted in the com-
position of a song, a story perhaps worth recounting.
Every year, in the late spring, the vineplants, which
begin then to grow their large leaves and sinewy
branches, need pruning. This the men do rapidly and
with great precision. As I said before, I attempted
this work under Jules's guidance and did it with great
imprecision. However, one aspect of pruning could
be done by any unskilled worker—even someone like
myself. The French word for that job is *épamprer*. The
dictionary says *épamprer* means *to prune,* but that is
not exact. When the leaves begin to grow on the
vineplant, the trunk of the plant itself sprouts small
leaves and branches. These divert precious sap from

the main stems, and from the grapes, and must be lopped off. By hand. That is what *épamprer* means precisely, and it is basic, hard work.

I was offered this work by Madame Basselier. She had heard, through someone else in the village, that I wanted work, and she sent word that I should come and see her. At that point, Iggy and I needed money, and so I was grateful for the job, and the thirty francs an hour—about five dollars—that I would earn. Iggy was working in the fields then, too, harvesting asparagus and collecting the same amount. The money I made in the Basseliers' fields was well earned. Up and down the long rows in the vineyard I'd go, bent over and duck-walking, ripping off leaves and branches from the trunk as fast as I could, trying hard to keep up with the workers in the rows alongside me. It was hot in St. Sébastien by then. I would steal a glance now and then to see how close to the end of the row I was. Once there, I'd have a precious minute or so to stand up, wipe my face, and take a swig of water.

After two or three weeks of this work, I decided to express my feelings by composing a song. I wrote "L'Épamprer blues." The song had its local and world premiere in the Basseliers' vineyard, where I sang it in front of Madame Basselier, Roland and several other French workers, to mixed reviews. This is the first verse. I will spare you the rest.

Je me suis levé ce matin
Et j'avais la gueule de bois.
Je me suis levé ce matin
Et j'avais la gueule de bois.
Mais quand même il faut épamprer
Jusqu'à six heures moins le quart.

I got up this mornin'
And my head felt so bad.
Yeah, I got up this mornin'
And my head it felt so bad.
But you know I still had to *épamprer*
Till five forty-five.

I sang my song in front of most of the village, too. It was at a party we gave at our house, near the end of our stay in St. Sébastien. The party was our way of saying goodbye. Everyone seemed to enjoy the song, but I never received any additional requests to sing. Jules, however, has written me nearly a year later to say, "We've finished *l'épamprage,* and so I'm not singing Richard's "Épamprer blues" any more." So maybe a few people remember it. I can still see Madame Basselier's face, her look of wonderment, as I serenaded the workers in her vineyard.

Madame Basselier grew up in the nearby city of Alès, but despite her urban background, she worked in the fields as hard as any man—harder than some. I could hardly keep up with her, whether we were lopping off aberrant leaves or planting melon seeds— another job she gave me. I was amazed that she never wore a hat, even in the searing August sun. That was inconceivable to me. Nevertheless there she was, planting, tearing, hacking or digging, her curly auburn hair facing the sun unprotected. She had a grown and married son named Augustin, who worked along with us, a quiet man with a splintery cough and stained fingers acquired from chainsmoking. Despite the fact that she was indeed a grandmother, I loved to look at her. I couldn't help it. She was so exuberant and so pretty.

After we had finished planting, Madame Basselier gave me about ten melon seeds. "They're expensive, Richard," she said, doling out the seeds one by one from her hand to mine. "And," she said, smiling at me, "I've given you the *American* variety. They are the best. Even better than the French variety!" She pointed a finger at me when she said that.

"Thank you, Madame," I said, looking down at the seeds resting in my hand, as if they were the magic seeds from "Jack and the Beanstalk." "That's very kind of you."

I liked the idea of having *melons* in my garden. They would add a touch of the exotic, which was good.

I took the seeds home with me in a small tin can. They were shaped much like sunflower seeds, only thinner, and they had been coated with an orange substance to protect them against disease. The film rubbed off easily, and after a day's planting in the

Basseliers' fields, my fingers were the color of a pumpkin. Like Jack of the fairy tale, I kept my seeds in the house overnight. But every once in a while that evening I took the can off the shelf and looked at them. They fascinated me. Seeds. To Madame Basselier, they were a means to an end, and a costly one. To me, they were incomprehensible. Why should I be amazed by a computer or a CAT scanner or an astronaut? What are they to a sliver of inert matter that contains within it the history of the world and the generations to come, as well?

The next day I went to the garden and planted the melons the way the Basseliers had taught me. I placed a narrow sheet of plastic over a mound of earth I had prepared. Then I opened a fist-sized hole about every fifteen inches in the plastic. I poured in a little water, let it soak in, then placed a single seed into each hole. I covered up the seed with a small amount of dirt, and that was that. The plastic provided a sort of hothouse effect, and because of the pent-up humidity, the seeds never required another watering. As Roland Basselier had told me, now I could leave them alone.

My little mound was just off to the side of the strictly-spaced rows of vegetables in my garden. Whenever I visited the garden to work and check on the progress of my plants, I looked first to see if my melon seeds had done anything. They were the most exciting thing in my garden to me, and the one

I wanted most to succeed—except, perhaps, for my tomatoes.

For the longest time, nothing happened. A few weeks passed, then more. I began to wonder if my seeds had died. (Can a seed die?) So I went to Roland and asked him if I needed to worry.

"This is a bad year for melons, Richard," he said. "Even ours are not doing well."

We were standing outside his house, next to the edge of his vineyard, which, in fact, literally went up to his front door. It was lunch time, and I could hear something sizzling on his kitchen stove. He offered me a *pastis,* but I refused. It was too hot.

"You mean," I said, "your melons are not growing?"

"Not much. Not much." Roland was a weathered, dark-haired man who looked a little like the fifties movie star Gilbert Roland—funny they should have that name in common! He had the same rough manliness about him, though unlike the movie star, he was weary-looking. While his wife was serious when she worked, Roland was easy and chatty. He surprised me with his knowledge of books. In the fields, bent over and hacking away in the sun, we would talk about Dumas, Zola, Hugo.

"What's wrong with the melons?" I asked.

"I don't know," he said. "We have had an expert from Montpellier here."

"What did he say?"

"Not much. He gave us some ideas. But really nothing has helped."

It was both comforting and saddening to know that Roland and I shared the same problem, though his was obviously far more serious. But even though he was facing the possible loss of part of his melon crop—his other varieties were doing all right—Roland never complained about this, or about any other catastrophe. Even when, earlier in the year, he had lost an entire field of seeds because someone had left the slightest trace of chemicals in the huge tank from which they took their water, he didn't say a word. He simply went and replanted the seeds, one by one.

"What should I do, Roland?" I pressed. "What are *you* going to do?"

"Nothing, Richard. Wait. I think they'll come. But they won't be very big, or very good."

My plants finally did grow. Before I knew what a melon plant actually looked like, I guess I had expected the melons to grow on a bush, or tree, like an orange. I don't know why. But they didn't, of course. First, a cloverlike sprout emerged from the hole in the plastic. This became more substantial; then, at one spectacular point, it divided in two, each half trailing down one side of the mound. Eventually, the tentacles grew longer and reached far beyond the mound. It was really like a pumpkin or watermelon, how they grew.

Soon enough, a small flower bloomed jutting out from the stem. Then several more just like it bloomed, each one falling off when a tiny, pale-green orb appeared to take its place. I thought, I really do have a melon plant.

But, despite my hope, my melons never were to be very large. They were stunted versions of themselves. In fact, most of the melons Iggy and I ate that summer in St. Sébastien were given to us by the Basseliers—the French variety, I guess—and by Jules. Another failure! I had wanted so much for this plant to do well. That it didn't was a bitter pill to swallow.

I had somehow believed the fact that lovely Madame Basselier herself had given me the seeds— had literally dropped them into my hand with her enticing smile, not to mention with those words, spoken in that sing-song Midi accent—would work together to bring me luck. What better blessing could I ask? But it wasn't to be. I guess, like Roland, I had to look beyond all this. I hadn't expected it, but in the end I was to have a deeper link to Roland Basselier than to his wife. He and I had now a failure in common. Mine stung. His damaged. But the point—what he showed me—was to accept it quietly. With nature, it was nothing personal.

 INSTINCTS

I RECOMMEND THAT ALL bachelors have a garden. It will give them, in some small way, the experience of being a parent. I make analogies to sex
and birth and children when I talk about a garden because they come naturally. In a garden, you put your
seeds into the earth, into the mother earth. They ger-
minate, they grow, they flower—like children. After
they begin to grow, you worry about them, you tend
them constantly, you fret over their maladies. Some
are stronger, bigger and healthier than others. That
concerns you. And mystifies you.

I reacted to my garden strongly, and in ways I

hadn't foreseen. At various moments, I felt responsible, protective, anxious, proud. I also felt mournful, impotent, defiant and lost. I remember once when my tomato plants were sick. Or at least they looked sick to me. Their leaves were withered and curled and hung limply all down the long stems, no longer the vivid things they used to be. In my anxiousness, I went about the village and sought the advice of men I knew, and I also went and talked to some I hadn't met before—something I would have been too shy to do before I had a garden. But my connection made the indulgence of shyness impossible. I had sick plants. I needed to make them well.

These men took my problem seriously, but they ended up confounding me. I'll never forget talking to them in the square in a small shaded area next to the town hall on a hot July afternoon. These men of the earth, doctors of the soil, gave me conflicting diagnoses and advice.

When I presented my situation to them, Albin Polge, the husky, near-sighted farmer who happened also to be the mayor of St. Sébastien, asked me, "Did you treat your plants, Richard?"

"Yes, yes," I said. "With sulphur."

"You mean," he said, taking off his glasses and wiping the telescope-thick lenses, "you didn't use sulphite, too?"

"*Sulphite?* Don't you mean sulphur?"

"No. No. Sulphite. You must use it." He put his

glasses back on. Then he looked at me carefully. "That may be the problem. A sickness."

Several of the men nodded along with his words.

"No, no," Monsieur Massot said to Albin. "It's not that." Monsieur Massot was a short, mustached man with a soft, word-caressing voice. He was a retired railroad worker who lived at the edge of the village with his wife, and he had a large garden. I used to pass by it on my walks, and I would often talk to him about the things he was growing. His advice was to be reckoned with. He turned from Albin to me. "It's the sun, Richard. The heat has dried all the leaves. It's happened before." He raised his eyebrows upward. "The sun is much too strong this year."

Even as he spoke, the sun's great heat penetrated into our shaded area. The only place where you were safe was inside the houses, behind the thick, cooling walls of stone.

"But," I said desperately, "can't I do anything about it?"

"No. Nothing," he said, with a kind of papal finality.

I couldn't accept that. "Not even if I water a lot more?"

"No." He shook his head. "It's too late."

I groaned.

"But don't worry, Richard," he said. "It won't harm your tomatoes. They will still come."

"Are you sure?"

"Yes. Certain."

As these men disagreed—there was even a third hypothesis about the type of soil I had—I remember feeling edgy and wondering, Can't you villagers agree *for once*? We're talking about my tomato plants!

My garden brought out a stronger instinct in me. Protectiveness. Those who feel a general love of all animals, or who are against the abuse of animals, should have a garden. They might modify their views. I remember one morning—and this after my garden was quite far along and very pretty, too— I found traces of a mole, *une taupe*. His tunneling wove in and out of my lettuce plants crazily, like a drunken driver. Apparently he had eaten nothing, because all the plants were still there, sitting in a row, healthy. (As Iggy said, "Maybe he didn't realize it was a garden.") But seeing that long, narrow mound of disturbed earth next to my plants ignited me. I thought, If I ever catch him (how, in God's name?), you can forget about the ASPCA—or whatever they call it here in France—I will personally bash his brains in. He will *not* wreck my garden.

And I would have killed him, too. Without remorse. Now, I suppose there may be methods by which you can keep a mole out of your garden without resorting to murder. But I didn't care. At that moment, protecting my garden was more important to me than saving his mangy little French hide, and I wasn't going to go out of my way to insure his well-being over that of my plants. And that was what made the feeling so exciting and free of moral doubt: it was an instinct.

Sometimes my instincts not only surprised me, they made me laugh, too. On my way to the garden one morning, I spotted a pile of horse manure on the road, a product of some adventurer from the riding stable in the nearby village of Boissac. Without hesitating—without thinking, really—I stopped the car, scooped the flaky, brown lumps into my bucket and zoomed off. Had I no pride? Not when it came to my garden. This stuff was *gold*. Pure gold. I'm sure no bird of prey could have been more satisfied bringing the chewed-up carcass of a field mouse to its fledglings than I did when I arrived with my bucketful of manure. I remember saying aloud to my plants: "Have I got something special for you today. *C'est la merde.*"

When you have a garden, you constantly ask yourself, like a parent, the questions *why?* and *why not?* I remember one eggplant, small and emaciated—it never really was healthy—was about to give up the ghost. I slowly uprooted it; it dangled in my hand, already dead. And just down the row, eggplants I had planted at the same time, bought from the same nursery, were big and strong as American farm boys. Why? Or, why *it,* and not them? Was it me? Was it the soil? Was it the weather? Disease? Insects? I never did find out. No matter how much I cared, I wasn't omnipotent. Eventually, I just had to accept.

The garden taught me that not only wasn't I all-knowing or all-powerful, but that it was a mistake to try to be. I could put the seeds into the ground. I could water. I could fertilize. I could grate. I could weed. But that was about it. The rest was up to them. Sometimes that was hard to accept. I had to be constantly *doing* something for, or to, my plants. I couldn't accept the idea that every bit of progress wasn't in some small measure due to me. Or to put it another way, I couldn't believe that my plants could, for long stretches at a time, do without me. And very well. I have seen meddling parents behave much the same way toward their children. Sometimes you have to let go.

All the while I felt protective toward my plants, but once they began producing their ripe fruit, my attitude changed. In a sense, my job was done. I had given and now I was ready to receive. Gardening is, in its perfect state, a true give-and-take relationship. Along with this natural shift came a different set of feelings, none of them less strong. This final hour produced moments of great glory. I remember the time when I could count on something being ripe, and ready to pick, every day. And when I could get up in the morning knowing that after I went to the garden I would have something to bring to Iggy. That

165

was a wonderful feeling. It was primitive, and it went very deep. It wasn't stronger than the urge to defend what was mine, but in a sense it was more profound, a calm, masculine instinct, resonating from my soul.

I remember, early on in the gathering process, returning from the garden one morning with a bucketful of vegetables—lettuce, cucumber, tomatoes, zucchini, even a small melon. Driving back to the village, I glanced over at the many-colored bounty from time to time, just for pleasure. That glance was the reward of months of labor. When I came home, Iggy had a cup of coffee for me and a piece of fresh, buttered bread. I showed her the vegetables, many still caked with damp earth. "Oh, *great!*" she said, her eyes wide with excitement. She smiled her open, sunny smile and came to me, putting her arms around my sweaty shoulders. I sat down and took a sip of the coffee. I felt proud. I was a provider.

 BOUNTY

AFTER WEEKS AND WEEKS of struggling away, of grooming and pampering, of digging, weeding, grating and watering, my garden was going to give. I could hardly contain myself. This was what it was all about, wasn't it? When I finally arrived one day to see, emerging from the crisp dryness of a former flower, my first tomato, a tiny, tough green orb and my first zucchini, a little green finger, I was happy beyond words.

Firsts. My first string beans, long, slim, supple things, all a pale green that seemed the essence of health to me. My first eggplant, poking its dark crimson noggin through a bud. There it was, that famous, slick burgundy skin! And coming from that same skinny plant Iggy and I had put into the ground months ago on a wet, cold April day. With sights like these, my eyes would open wide, and the adrenaline would race through my body. It was all happening in the garden then, an unstoppable unfolding, an explosion. I could practically *hear* it all growing. Sometimes it was hard to keep up with, and sometimes I'd nearly miss some event—a new cucumber hidden by its own fat leaves, a second pepper nearly obscured by its identical neighbor.

On those mornings in mid and late summer in France, I couldn't wait to go to the garden. It was the stage when everything was magnificent. When I could do some weeding in the morning and return in the evening to find that a vegetable had visibly grown, that a tomato had turned color, become a red adult within a matter of sun-drenched hours. Or a zucchini might seem to have doubled its size. And the moment when I took my first ripe tomato home, cutting and eating it—one half for Iggy, one half for me—that was an occasion. Photographs had to be taken then. There were many moments like this, and they were made much of.

Ultimately, there came a day when the garden was groaning with its own bounty. (For weeks, everything seemed to be happening so slowly; now it was happening amazingly fast.) Now each trip meant I would fill my green rubber bucket with wonderful ripe things: flaming peppers, tomatoes, vibrant green lettuce, parsley, cucumbers. I loved cutting the vegetables from their stems, releasing them from their green tethers and putting them into my bucket, hearing the *plop* as they hit the bottom. And to pluck a huge tomato with the merest touch, hold it, weighty and juicy, in my hands—that act carried me the whole morning. I was so full of contentment then. Resolution was everywhere.

When I picked my very first two vegetables from the garden, I knew just what I was going to do with them. They were two medium-sized cucumbers. I put them in my green rubber bucket and drove back to St. Sébastien. This was a moment to be savored, a proud moment. I drove back on the little French road, wheeling my Peugeot back and forth with one hand, stepping on the gas. Just before the huge *cave coopérative,* I turned into a familiar driveway. I pulled to a halt. A figure emerged from the house to see who it was: Madame Favier, Jules Favier's mother. It was noon, on a lovely late June day.

Madame Favier was a tiny woman, bursting with energy, such an unlikely mother of four tall, lanky sons. When she drove their big, clanky station wagon, her head seemed barely to rise above the steering wheel. Her name was Marie-Rose. She came from Calais, in the north of France, and she and Jules's father, Gilbert, had met at a Catholic Youth

Conference, something I always found terribly sweet. She had a high, excited voice and a ready smile, and she always made me feel welcome.

"Good day, Madame," I said to her.

"Marie-Rose! Not Madame!" she said, smiling at me and wiping her hands with a dish towel. She, like all the women in the village, was always working.

"Good day . . . Marie-Rose," I said. "How are you?" Because of the formality of the French language, I always had difficulty calling villagers by their first names, even when they asked me to.

"Oh, *ça va, ça va*," she said dismissively. All right. All right. No one said that simple, noncommittal phrase with more implied meaning than she.

"Is your husband—is Gilbert here?"

"Yes, yes. He's inside."

"May I see him?"

"Of course. *Gilbert!*" she shouted at the house. "Come out! Richard is here."

Gilbert Favier came out. He was tall, taller even than his sons, an improbable-looking farmer with thinning hair, a kind of academic air and spectacles. He was a great *pétanque* player—that game of tossed steel balls you see Frenchmen playing in parks throughout the land—a good, kind man, and very amusing. He was always teasing and joking. He cared very much for his children. I could see why Jules had turned out to be such a good man.

"Good day, Gilbert," I said to him.

"Good day, Richard. How goes the garden?" We were standing in his driveway. Off to the side, near the road, was a large oak tree. Underneath it were at least fifteen *pétanque* balls, weathered and dark gray from use.

"Ah, it's good that you ask," I said to the man who had lent me the land where I had made my garden. "I have something for you."

I took out the cucumbers from the bucket and handed them to him.

"From the garden?" Marie-Rose said, coming closer and peering.

"Yes!" I gleamed proudly.

Gilbert smiled. He began to hand them back to me. "You keep them, Richard. They're for you." He put them back into my hands.

I knew it! I knew it would be almost impossible to make him accept my token of gratitude for the gift of his land. In St. Sébastien, it was so much easier to receive from the villagers than it was to give to them. Often, you had to twist their arms to get them to accept any little gift. And Gilbert Favier was a very persistent and very clever refuser. He might have been the best refuser in the entire village. He had an air of deniability about him that was nearly impossible to penetrate. But it was important to me that he take the cucumbers, superfluous as they might be. I wanted at least one opportunity to thank him on my own terms.

"You must take the cucumbers, Gilbert. They are the first things from my garden."

"Richard," he said, looking at my offering, "we have plenty of things from our own garden. And what we don't have, we can get from my father's garden." His father—the grandfather Jules adored—had an immense garden near the river. It was true, they did have everything.

I stammered. I hesitated. I panicked. Then, seemingly from nowhere, came inspiration.

"In *America*," I said as solemnly as I could and standing a bit straighter, "this is what we do. When someone loans someone some land, uh, it is a sort of . . . tradition to give the person who loaned you the land your first vegetables." It sounded crazy even to me.

"Oh," he said. He looked at his wife. She shrugged her shoulders.

"So, please, you must take them."

"Well . . ."

"Here."

He took the cucumbers. They looked pretty puny in his enormous hands.

"Thank you," he said dubiously as he looked at them.

"I hope they taste good," I said.

In the village of St. Sébastien de Caisson, there were many rituals, big and small. Some were subtle, woven nearly seamlessly into the fabric of village life, and I'm sure I may have missed a few of them. I tried to learn and adhere to as many as I could. I knew they were important. But I never pretended I was a Frenchman. I wasn't dissatisfied with who I was. I had my own rituals, too. And they might not understand them.

I got into the car and drove out of the driveway. I turned onto the road and headed toward my house. I looked into the rearview mirror and saw Gilbert and Marie-Rose turn and walk back to the house. The cucumbers had completely disappeared into the vastness of Gilbert's hand. Such a delightful couple!

I shifted gears, the little engine whined.

I have a color photograph of myself on my wall in New York that was taken by a friend. I am in our house in St. Sébastien, in the kitchen. The sunlight, even indoors, is intense, rich. I am holding a head of lettuce in my hand. I am holding it before me, and I am looking at it and smiling. It is lettuce I have grown myself, in my own garden. It is one of those soft, densely packed heads, the leaves of which you find in salads in most bistros in France. We probably ate it with our lunch that day—at least I hope we did—with a little olive oil and perhaps a splash of lemon. And perhaps with it, some slices of tomato, bleeding with summer, also taken from the garden.

173

And since the photograph was taken by a friend, it's certain that he, and maybe some others, shared that meal with us, seated around our long wooden table, the windows thrown open, letting the summer air stream in. Wine, bread, cheese, water, meat, salad before us all.

 LEAVING

 # DRUMS

JULES CAME BY the house one hot August afternoon to announce, "Madame Flanet has said she will
lend you three large drums."

Drums, or *bidons,* were empty oil drums in which
I could store water from the river to water my plants.
My stream was nearly dry, and I needed some kind of
reserve.

"Great! Who is Madame Flanet?" I asked Jules.
We were sitting at the table in the dining room of our
stone house. I had just finished lunch. The remains of
the meal were scattered on the table: paté—heavy for
August, but so good—tomato slices, cheese, crusty

bread, fruit. I offered Jules a *pastis*. He refused. He hardly ever took any refreshment I offered, and when he did, it was usually simply an orange drink, which I offered him now.

"She," Jules said, referring to Madame Flanet, "lives in Mejannes-Sarden. She's a friend of my mother. They go to the same church together."

"Oh. And she'll lend me *three* drums?"

"Yes."

"Does she know I'm an American?"

"No. Why should she care about something like that?"

"Oh, I don't know. I guess . . . well, never mind." I was just curious. I leaned forward. "When can we go and get the drums?"

The windows were open. The whole force of the August day pulsed into the room.

"We can go anytime," Jules said. "I just need to telephone her first to tell her we will be coming."

Mejannes-Sarden! This trip would *extend* my garden. It was about ten kilometers away—a charming little village. True, I had gone to Nîmes to buy seeds and tools, but other than that, I had looked to St. Sébastien for answers to any problems in my garden. Now I would be traveling distances to help save its life.

"Fantastic," I said. "By the way, thanks, Jules. Thanks once again."

He gave me his famous dismissive, almost disdainful, look—the one that he always gave me when I said "thank you" for a favor. I smiled. I knew him too well. He got up to go.

"To work," he said. Then, before he went, he glanced at the table and the scatterings of the meal. He looked at the clock.

"Don't you ever eat your lunch at a normal time?" he asked me. In the small villages, people began their midday meal at the stroke of twelve.

"This *is* normal, Jules. In America, one-thirty *is* normal.

"This is not America. This is France," he said.

"You're right, Jules. What can I say?"

He shook his head hopelessly and left, closing the wooden door behind him. I guess I was beyond redemption.

Drums! I would have *bidons*. They each held 250 liters. I would have water. Help was on the way! And I needed it. I waited eagerly for Jules to call Madame Flanet to arrange for a time to go to her house in Mejannes-Sarden.

Early in the morning, two days later, he came by in his car on his way to work in the vineyards. He told me we could go to Madame Flanet's house that day at noon if I was willing.

"Yes. Terrific," I said.

"Good," Jules said, leaning his head out of his car window. "I will come by at noon."

Jules came at noon precisely, as he always did when

he made an appointment for that hour. It was a searingly hot day. When I asked him about lunch, he said he had already eaten. I got into his car, and we drove out of St. Sébastien toward St. Paul les Fonts, the next village, some three kilometers away. Then it was on to Mejannes-Sarden, another five or six kilometers. As usual, Jules drove very fast, and the dust rose up behind us in swirls.

I loved the road, D140, from St. Sébastien to Mejannes-Sarden. It was narrow and winding and passed over small bridges and by empty stone houses and vineyards and occasional clusters of green oak trees. It was everything I could ever want in a country road in France. After one or two kilometers of driving, Jules broke the silence to tell me about Madame Flanet.

"She has had a difficult time," he said, glancing out at the fields. His left arm rested on the open window.

"How do you mean?" I asked him.

He paused, turned his head to look and inspect a vineyard we passed—I never knew what he looked for—then said, "Her husband tried to kill her."

"*What?*" This was such an incredible statement, I wasn't sure he had said what he said. I went over the French words one by one in my mind again to reassure myself. Then I wasn't certain how to react. In nearly a year of living in St. Sébastien, I'd never heard of anything like this.

"Really?" I said to him. "What happened?"

"He tried to strangle her."

"My God! What did she do?"

Jules gave me each piece of information sparingly, as if he were feeding a parakeet. "She escaped. She ran into her bedroom and locked the door. Then she called the police."

"How did she escape?"

"I don't know. This was not the first time he had been violent to her."

The heat poured into the open windows. We drove along in silence for a few minutes. Because it was noon, there were no other cars on the road. All the people were at home, eating. I found this information very disturbing, mainly because, since I was borrowing the drums, it was now associated with my garden.

Jules then added casually, "When the police came, they found the man in the garage." He turned to look at me briefly. "Dead."

"*Dead?* How?"

"He had shot himself. With his rifle."

Although Jules told me this story respectfully, there was something in him—I could tell—that enjoyed exposing the macabre to me.

With this story, I felt a mixture of pity and astonishment for Madame Flanet. In a way, I no longer wanted to go to her place. But I saw we had turned off the main road and were obviously coming near.

"Does she live nearby?" I asked Jules.

"The house is just here." He motioned ahead with a flick of his eyes. I suddenly wondered:

"Jules, when did all this happen?"

"Last Tuesday." He turned and looked at me.

Before I had a chance to—what? choke?—Jules turned into her driveway, and there was Madame Flanet, standing at her gate waiting for us.

We stopped the car, got out and walked over to her. She was in a long cream summer dress, a not-unattractive woman in her fifties with a sad, kind face. She spoke softly, and when she realized I was American—this *was* apparently news to her—she expressed only the mildest surprise. I was instantly drawn to her. She was the kind of Frenchwoman I adored, soft, yet strong from working outdoors.

She led us to the drums. They were in her backyard. She had a fair-sized stone house—not ancient like mine—in the typical one-story style of the region. She had an unlimited view of the vineyards, however, and there was just one other house in the vicinity with which to share it.

The drums were filled with sand, for some reason. We had to empty them into a large container with big scoops she provided us. This took ten minutes or so. Madame Flanet stood quietly nearby, in the shade of a tree. I stole glances at her from time to time. All the while, as Jules and I shoveled scoop after scoop after rhythmical scoop, my mind could not help but go back to last Tuesday. I imagined her husband's hands around her neck. Violent, unthinkable words. A furious struggle. His trying to *kill* her. Screams. A desperate escape. A flight to the house, to the bedroom. Tears. A nearly incomprehensible call to the police. Sirens. Voices. A shot.

Madame Flanet showed nothing of this, nothing. She stood there calmly, a slight breeze blowing the bottom of her dress backward.

We finished emptying the drums of the sand and then hauled them over to Jules's car. Before we began to load them into the back, Madame Flanet asked us to come to the garage. The garage! We walked inside. It was a cool, small, dark place. This was where they found him after he had killed himself. I didn't like being there.

"Do you need any gardening tools?" she asked me and pointed.

Lined up against the wall was everything I could possibly have wanted: shovels, rakes, hoes, all kinds of things, all in beautiful condition. What a trove! How sad I couldn't use them, that I already had my things.

"I used to have a garden," she told me. "In the back yard. It was mostly flowers. But, well, I can't manage now."

As she spoke, I hurriedly lowered my eyes to look for any traces of blood on the floor, of brains. But I couldn't find any. Less than seven days ago, there was

183

a dead man sprawled out here, maybe exactly where I was standing—maybe not even dead at that point.

"Please, take what you want. Anything," she said.

"No, no, thank you, Madame," I said. "I have everything I need. Really."

"Very well," she said.

We walked outside into the sun. She closed the garage door carefully. Jules and I went back to his car and loaded the three drums into the back of his car. It was a slightly complicated process. Finally, they were situated, and it was time to go. I was about to thank Madame Flanet when she said,

"Monsieur, if you know of anyone who might be interested in buying a house, please have them contact me." She, like everyone else here, knew that foreigners, especially British and American, were always searching for houses to buy in the south of France.

"You want to sell your house?" Jules asked her. This interested him for some reason.

"Yes," she said. "It's . . . too big for me. I can't manage anymore."

"Where will you go?" Jules asked.

"Oh, I don't know. Probably to Alès. My daughter lives there. I'll buy an apartment there."

Madame Flanet had been looking out at the vineyards. Now she turned back and looked at us. I looked into her eyes. I wasn't sure I wanted to look too deeply. I didn't know what to say to her with my eyes. She smiled briefly. It was a nice smile, quite captivating. "Well, anyway, if you hear of anything," she said.

"Yes, of course, Madame," Jules said to her.

"Thank you so much, Madame," I said. "This will be a *big* help for me."

"It's nothing," she said. "I am happy to help."

We got into the car. As Jules backed up and turned onto the road, I looked at her over the three drums in the car that rose up and nearly blocked the view. Madame Flanet closed the gate to her yard and turned to go to her house. The last I saw of her was her back, her long pale dress. The dust from Jules's car obscured her figure somewhat. I turned back around. I looked at Jules. He was occupied with his driving. On this monstrously hot day, in the full blast of the noon August sun, I shivered as if I were freezing cold.

 RABBITS

I PULLED MY CAR up next to Albin Polge's stone house, which was just around the corner from the small Catholic church. (There was even a Protestant *temple* in St. Sébastien, too. In a village of just 211 people!) Albin's house had a nice balcony, and it was heavily adorned with ivy and flaming flowers. Strangely, I never saw Albin, St. Sébastien's mayor for the past sixteen years, enter or leave his house. I got out of the car and took my green bucket with me. It was a warm August morning, too early yet to be uncomfortable. I walked down the shaded stoneway between the houses. Sun splashed everywhere, mixing with the shade agreeably. The early air was very sweet. A few villagers were chatting outside. They said hello to me and I to them. I reached the Vasquezes' house, a place where Iggy and I had spent many hours. I put my bucket down and knocked on the door.

"*Oui?*" Madame Vasquez's voice came timidly from within. If she didn't know who was outside, and especially if her husband wasn't at home, her tone was suspicious when you knocked on her door. Madame Vasquez was afraid of gypsies, among other potential intruders, who, she said, always knew somehow when your husband wasn't home. She once told us— her voice quaking with fear even as she spoke— about the time gypsies came to her door and angrily demanded money. "I don't have any money!" she had said to them from her second-story window, in tears. "No money! No money!" Then she had hidden herself—in a closet, I think. Eventually, the gypsies went away. But not before they had threatened her. I never saw any gypsies in St. Sébastien, but I certainly believed her story.

"It's me. Ricardo!" I shouted as reassuringly as I could.

"*Vengo!*" she shouted back. I'm coming!

I heard a slow clomp of footsteps as she descended the stairs. Then the beautiful, heavy oak door opened. I never knew how they could afford such a luxury, this fabulous door, which was so appropriately Spanish. Madame Vasquez emerged. I could see her *cave* in the background, the rooms that contained the shelves laden with canned fruits and vegetables and the little city of potatoes scattered on the floor.

"Señor Ricardo, good day," she said. She was dressed totally in black today. With her black hair and dark eyes, her sombre dress, I was transported to Spain.

"Good day, Señora. You must call me Ricardo, not Señor."

"Si, Señor," she said seriously. Then, realizing what she had said, she closed her eyes and her body shook with laughter.

"Señora," I said, "I've got something for you from the garden."

"Your garden?" she said, and she leaned over slightly, trying to peer into the bucket. "Good. Good." Even though she at first had resisted, I had worked out an agreement with her that she would accept a few things from me, from the garden.

I took out a head of lettuce. There were three more just like it in the bucket. I handed it to her.

"Lettuce," I said. "For you."

She took the head and turned it around in her hand quickly.

"*Gracias,*" she said without apparent enthusiasm.

"No good?" I said, my face vulnerable in the face of judgment.

"Yes," she said. Then she arched her head upward, toward her terrace. "For the rabbits."

"Oh," I said. My face flushed. The word *rabbits* rang in my ear. I hoped no one else could hear what she had said.

But the truth was, my lettuce wasn't so good. I had deceived myself as to its quality, hoping it was better than it really was. Maybe I'd had too many disappointments lately in the garden.

"Yes," Madame Vasquez said. "This lettuce is very good for the rabbits." She picked at it expertly. "They will like it. *Gracias.*"

The Vasquezes raised rabbits up on their terrace. Normally, they had about six or seven at one time. They raised them for food. Madame Vasquez had in fact killed one for us once. Before the execution, she had taken Iggy and me upstairs to see our future meal in person. I remember looking at the rabbit, watching his nose rapidly working, looking into his whiskered face and moon eyes, and thinking, "He knows!" But we let her go ahead. I remember the next day taking the rabbit home in a paper bag, the pale, flayed body still sticky with blood. It was huge and delicious. I somehow managed to obliterate my guilt, what little remained.

Now, as I said, it was a bit humiliating to have my produce judged not fit for human consumption. Madame Vasquez hadn't even waited a beat to say: *For the rabbits.* Actually, I had gathered much delicious lettuce from the garden in earlier weeks. But lately, with the menacing heat, the lettuce had become listless, sour and tough. She was right, and I knew it. It wasn't good. I wasn't trying to fool her. I was trying to fool myself.

"Please," she said, "bring any other lettuce you have." Her eyes shot upward toward the terrace.

I handed her the three remaining heads. She took them happily. "*Gracias,*" she said.

"And your garden, Señora?" I said.

"Oh, *mucho trabajo,*" she said, fanning her face with her hand.

"Yes, but is it coming along?"

"*Ça va,*" she said. It goes.

I said goodbye and walked back up to my car. It was still a beautiful day, not so hot. So, I was feeding her rabbits now. Working hard at it, too! It was interesting, I thought, this whole gardening bit. You try to keep rabbits out of your garden, in any way you can. And then you find yourself asking them to come right in, as it were, and go at it. Well, so what? I had eaten one of them. I guess I owed them something.

 HEAT

NOW, ALL I SEEM TO remember is the heat. The heat, and how it scorched the land and made it hard as an iron plate and stunted, even finally killed, the vegetables I was trying to grow. It was a savage, unrelenting heat, like that shocking exhalation that comes at you from a furnace door opened. But this heat could not be closed away by a door; it surrounded you, assaulted you, and made venturing into the open anytime after eleven A.M. without a hat truly foolhardy. I say "unrelenting" because, in fact, it did not rain except for one or two showers from June through August. That blasted heat! I was impotent against it. And I tried everything. I can understand now the wild logic of performing a rain dance. *Why not?* I needed rain so very badly for my garden. I was ready to beg for it from whoever, or whatever, would listen. Please—*give me rain.*

Il fait chaud. It's hot. That's all I heard, day in and day out. *Il fait chaud.* I grew sick and, finally, sad at heart to hear it spoken. Oh, the sick, the cracked, dried-up earth! Oh, *mon jardin.* I raised my fist in defiance to the sun, but it was a useless gesture.

Heat, heat, heat.

Now, it wasn't as if I hadn't expected it to get hot. Even as an American I knew, in April, when it was damp and cool, that it would eventually turn very warm. Yes, I knew summer would arrive as it always did. In fact, I was eager to see its face. Summer in the south of France. But one day early on in April when I told Monsieur Noyer about my garden for the first time, I have to admit I wasn't prepared for his response.

"Where is your land, Richard?" he asked me. We were standing in the middle of the town square, just the two of us, on a damp, gray day.

"Out past the big stone marker. The one that describes the battle." I pointed my hand in that direction. "It's just past the little bridge. Off to the side."

"By the river?" He cleared his throat and peered at me, his thick eyebrows rising upward.

"No. It's on the opposite side of the road."

"You have no *robinet*?" People with gardens by the river often installed a faucet with a pump to draw water.

"No," I said proudly.

"How do you get your water then?"

"Oh, I've got plenty of water!" I said to him. "There is a stream running nearby, right past the edge of the land."

"Oh? A stream?"

"Yes."

He whistled. Then he looked to his left. "We'll see, Richard," he said lowly. "We'll see how much water you have in that stream in the month of August."

I shrugged my shoulders and laughed. The stream was burly and energetic. What was he talking about? Of course I'd have water in August. Yet there was something cold and confident in the way he spoke. "*On verra le mois d'août.*" We'll see the month of August. These words lingered with me much longer than I would have liked.

I'm not sure exactly when my feelings about the sun and the heat turned from something like pleasure to worry (which itself ultimately became fear), but it must have been in June sometime. That's when it became hot in St. Sébastien. The exact temperature? Perhaps 95, perhaps more. I don't recall. At first, I thought we were experiencing a heat wave. Yes, a *wave* of heat that, like all waves, would soon enough crest and crash, allowing normal temperatures to resume. But like the whaler's wife who, from her New England parapet, searched the horizon every day for years, hoping to see a trace of a ship, or any sign of her husband's return, I waited in vain. And I deluded myself about the stark reality. The heat never broke. St. Sébastien just grew hotter and hotter. It came to a point where I was grateful that our house was made of thick stone. It was a refuge I would escape to; inside was a cool, sweet haven.

"Is this *normal,* this heat?" I would ask everyone in the village.

"Yes," they would answer. "It's normal. *C'est l'été.*" It's summer. But later even *they* changed their tunes.

The heat began to dry my land and bake it. It made ugly fissures in my garden, the sort you see on public television broadcasts about deserts. I could pour water into them endlessly, and it had no effect. There was something outrageous about that. At first, the heat didn't seem to affect my plants. My tomatoes burgeoned. Even my cucumber plants continued spreading their tentacles everywhere, thriving in the Mojave ground. But all that changed eventually. Leaves withered. Fruit was stunted. Whole plants died. In the end, the heat slaughtered most everything. I didn't have enough water to counteract the sun's force.

The entire month of July was frustrating. I knew that August would be hell, but if only I could get a small break in July. I dreamed about just one thing:

rain. I searched the sky continually for any sign of dark clouds. Clouds. Any trace of gray could produce the wildest speculation from me. But there weren't many. Damn the south of France and its picture-perfect weather! Searching the sky for rain clouds, I saw instead Canadair planes, those flying firefighters that could scoop up great quantities of water from the Mediterranean. Their bellies gorged, they moved slowly toward plumes of smoke to release their showers downward. The still anticipation of fire was everywhere then. This was slow murder, these temperatures, cruel and unusual punishment.

I now had to water later and later, because the sun didn't set until nine o'clock, or even nine-thirty. I'd reach down and touch the earth late in the evening and feel it still pulsating with heat. Only at dawn was the land cool. I'd drive by the other gardens and see how healthy they looked. They were being watered from *robinets*. I was jealous and, in my darkest, most anguished moments, spiteful. I had some of Cain in me, and I hated to see it emerge. But I knew how lovely and exuberant the things I had planted could be when they had plenty of water; it was distressing to see them so scrawny and so feeble. I couldn't provide for them. Try as I would, I couldn't.

I guess I hadn't done such a good job. But the sun! It consoled me somewhat to hear Gilbert Favier, Jules's father, say, "This is the hottest summer I have seen in St. Sébastien in many years, Richard."

Then one night it happened. It rained. It was

completely unexpected, a fine deluge, and oh, Lord, what a good sound. *Rain.* I couldn't wait to go and see the garden that next morning. I think I probably left the house before six A.M. And there it was, my land all covered with a brown dampness. All of it pitted throughout with tiny depressions from the rain. It looked like a large piece of pastry, supple and irregular. The humidity from the earth mixed with the morning heat to produce a tropical steaminess that was wonderful to work in. Everything looked content, well fed and serene. Even the remarkably hard and deep fissures were pliant. I could close them together, like skin. Sweat dripped down my chest as I dug into the earth. I worked until I was totally exhausted, digging and turning and crumbling the moist earth. Maybe there was hope after all.

When I returned that evening, the land was dry again. No! It was all gone, the rain's effect. The sun, in just a few hours, had dried it all up. What was this thing I was battling?

In August, my stream did indeed begin to dry up. Little by little at first, but then it was all too obvious. I tried to fool myself about it, but after a while that was fruitless. As the stream grew smaller and weaker, Monsieur Noyer's words rang in my ear like a curse from an Italian opera: *We'll see the month of August.* He was right. I panicked. How would I water my plants? Where would I get the water? At this point the land was drinking water greedily like an insatiable child. "You must now water three times a day," my newspaper salesman told me. He was an ardent gardener, this bitter, hard-working Frenchman, and I kept him informed on a daily basis of my little plot of land. Like every other gardener I met, he held hard opinions. Now, his three-times-a-day mandate only added to my panic. *How?* How was I going to find the water? My carrots and spinach were already choking and terminally ill. What was I going to do?

Once again, as I had on so many countless occasions, I turned to Jules Favier.

"Jules," I said to him when I found him at last, "what do I do now?"

"We will have to go to the river," he said calmly, as if he'd been expecting me at any moment. "That's why I told you you would need three drums from Madame Flanet. Remember, you said that two would be enough?"

"I did?"

"Certainly."

"Well . . . perhaps I might have said that. Anyway, how do we get water from the river?"

"How else? With a pump."

What we did next may seem excessive to some. But when you have fought and worked hard for something you love, you don't retreat, even in the face of so formidable an adversary as the sun. Retreat? The two of us never even discussed abandoning

197

the garden. The next afternoon after his work I met Jules at his house and we began a process that, except for the engines involved, was as ancient as farming the earth itself. We went searching for water.

Jules hooked a small flatbed to the back of his tractor. On it was a five-hundred-gallon tank of galvanized tin, battered and slightly lopsided. Next to it, he placed a kerosene-powered pump, small, greasy and heavy. We also had some old canvas fire hose. We started off for the river. I rode on back to keep the pump from falling off. It was a lovely ride, I remember, bumpy and slow. At the river, we backed the tractor to the edge, connected everything properly and started the pump. It spat and snorted, but it worked. The canvas hose became tumescent; the slightly fetid water from the river was drawn and gushed forcefully from the hose into the tank. I stood in the river, amongst all the reeds and wild plants, holding the hose and waiting. I liked being there. It was fresh and cool and alive. I was in the tan river up to my knees. Whenever I moved, I could feel sediment being stirred and see it swirling around my legs. I felt my soul refreshed. I never wanted to leave. But, in just ten minutes, the tank was full. *Water*. We had water.

"Great, Jules," I said happily. I *was* happy, too. Jules nodded and started the tractor engine. I disconnected the hose from the pump and put everything back on the flatbed. As we left, I looked back at the river and sighed. There was so much water there. Why couldn't there be a way where I could divert some of it to . . . ?

We got to the garden and filled the three *bidons,* the drums of Madame Flanet, with water. How lovely they looked full with their lakelike surfaces at the tops. Strange, big, multi-legged insects from the river treaded water in them. Then, with what remained in the large tank, we began to water the garden. The water flowed in great gushes down the little troughs I had cut next to my plants. The ground soaked it in quickly. But this time we had enough. More than enough. My garden drank gallon after gallon after gallon. The whole process took twenty minutes or so. Drink, I thought. Drink up!

I went over to Jules. My face and hands were caked with mud from directing the hose to the plants. After so many weeks of dryness, I liked the idea of mud in my garden. Jules had hopped down from the tractor and was standing there watching the water flow out. I didn't thank him this time. I hoped by this somehow he could be certain I would do the same for him, and more, if he ever needed anything. I stood by him in the dying day, watching contentedly. Was all this effort for a few string beans, a few tomato plants, some basil and lettuce, some zucchini and a few eggplants—all of which we could buy at a store so very cheaply and so easily?

Yes.

 LEAVING

THE TIME CAME to leave, as it always does, and so I had to say my goodbyes.

I don't always like to face saying goodbye. I put it off to the last minute, or I never really do it at all. Leaving hurts the heart, and I felt I had had too many leavings in France already. But living with Iggy and her fierce attachments to people had taught me the importance of standing up to the moments when we must say goodbye. And the garden had meant too much to me not to acknowledge its end with some form of ceremony. So the day before Iggy and I left the village for good, I went with Jules to the garden for the last time. To say goodbye.

Standing there, on the plateau for the final time, Jules next to me, my garden stretched out before me, many of my plants still alive—growing, even, in the wretched heat—was not easy. I had asked Jules to please look after my garden when I was gone, letting him know I was aware it was faltering and so he shouldn't worry about that too much.

"Take any tomatoes you want, Jules," I said. "Or anything else you want that's left."

"You don't have to worry about your garden," he said in his typical laconic way. Then as we stood there quietly for a few minutes, the sun beating down on the caked ground before us, he peered at the withering plants and said to me consolingly, "You have not had the best year in which to make your garden in France."

Still, the idea of complaining was unthinkable. I had had more than my share of good fortune. I had led a dream life for the year I was in France, and my garden had made it more remarkable. I had been so lucky. From that first bleak, cold day back in April when Jules and I stood outside my house in St. Sébastien, shuffling our feet on the ground, to the day in late August when I went to the sun-cracked earth and plucked the last ripe tomato off the vine, I'd led a charmed life. I'd gotten closer to France and to my village than I ever imagined I would. I'd learned. I'd had adventures. I'd done what I had dreamed about doing all my life, the work that had made me feel like a boy in Virginia again. How many people can say that? Yes, the heat. Yes, the failures. Yes, yes, all of that. But they were nothing compared to the great pleasures I'd had—my Peugeot 104, my green bucket, my shovel and grater, my old cap and the entire morning free in which to work like a demon in the open French air.

A few weeks after I'd returned to New York and recommenced my metropolitan life, I called Jules in France. He was pleased enough to hear from me, but slightly distracted, as usual. I knew he was listening carefully, though.

"Jules," I said to him, "how is the garden? You know I haven't been there in quite a while."

"Your garden is fine. Considering the heat, it is fine."

"But! But! I mean, how are my tomatoes? And what about my melons? Did they ever grow any more?"

"Your melons did not grow so much more."

"Oh. That's too bad. And what about the tomatoes?"

"You had some more. Not too many. I gave them all to Madame Flanet."

"Oh, Madame Flanet! Good. Thanks, Jules. I hope she liked them. And my lettuce?"

"Not really," he said. Then he paused. "Monsieur Noyer has been to your garden," he said.

"Monsieur *Noyer*? Really? He went to my garden? What did he say?"

"He said the sun had done its work. He said he had warned you. He said he told you you should never have a garden without a faucet, without enough water."

"I know he did! I know he said that! Yes, he was right, Jules. But what else could I do? I wanted to have a garden."

Jules said nothing to this.

"Did Monsieur Noyer say anything else, Jules?"

Jules took one of his famous pauses, then said, "He said you hadn't done too badly. For an American."